MW01169531

CARNE!

Meat Dishes the Italian Way

Text by Sara Vignozzi
Photography by Marco Lanza
Set Design by Sara Vignozzi

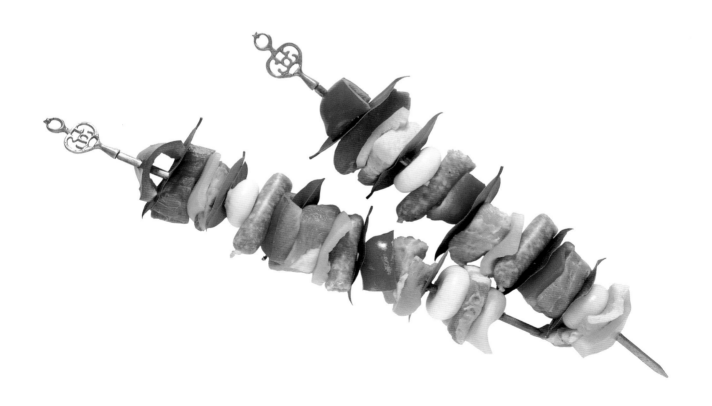

McRae Books

Other titles in the same series:
Pastissima! Pasta the Italian Way
Antipasti! Appetizers the Italian Way
Verdure! Vegetables the Italian Way
Zuppe Risotti Polenta! Italian Soup, Rice & Polenta Dishes
Pizza Pane Focacce! Pizza, Bread & Focacce the Italian Way
Pesce! Fish & Seafood the Italian Way
Dolci e Frutta! Deserts & Sweets the Italian Way

© 2001 McRae Books Srl, Florence (Italy)

Conceived, edited and designed by McRae Books
Series editors: Anne McRae, Marco Nardi

Text: Sara Vignozzi
Photography: Marco Lanza
Set Design: Sara Vignozzi
Design: Marco Nardi

Translation from the Italian: Darryl Price (Koiné)
Editing: Alison Leach, Lynn McRae, and Anne McRae
Illustrations: Paola Holguín
Color separations: Fotolito Toscana, Florence, Italy

The publishers would like to thank Mastro Ciliegia (Fiesole),
Eugenio Taccini (Montelupo Fiorentino), Flavia Srl (Montelupo Fiorentino),
La Tuscia (Lastra a Signa), Alessandro Frassinelli and Leonardo Pasquinelli
for their assistance during the production of this book.

All rights reserved. No part of this publication may be reproduced, stored
in a retrieval system, or transmitted in any form or by any means electronic,
mechanical, photocopying, recording or otherwise, without the prior
written permission of the copyright owner.

ISBN 88-88166-15-7

Printed and bound in Italy by Artegrafica, Verona

CONTENTS

INTRODUCTION

Meat dishes have never gone out of fashion in Italy. They are still an essential component of a balanced and well-orchestrated traditional meal. When preparing a special lunch or dinner, a resourceful cook will serve a tiny appetizer, followed by pasta, minestrone or risotto, both chosen with a careful eye to the all-important secondo piatto, which will almost certainly be based on meat. Whether it be a few succulent slices of roast pork or lamb, a sliver of veal braised in white wine, or a grilled Florentine steak, the overall effect will be harmonious and satisfying. The meat dish will be accompanied by a salad or a well chosen vegetable dish and each course will be served with a carefully selected wine. In keeping with these traditions, I have suggested a side dish and a wine for each recipe. For ease of consultation, the book has been divided into five chapters, according to the type of meats used. Chapter headings are: Turkey and Chicken, Veal and Beef, Lamb, Pork, and Game.

INGREDIENTS

A wide range of ingredients are used to prepare the recipes in this book. However, the majority are common and will already be on the shelves of most well-stocked kitchens. A point to remember about oil: always buy the highest quality extra-virgin oil to be found. Good olive oil is expensive in Italy too, but it is well worth it. Old or poor quality oil has a rancid taste that will spoil all the time and effort spent in preparing the dishes.

COARSE SEA SALT

SUGAR

HONEY

TEA

MUSTARD POWDER

CORNSTARCH (CORN FLOUR)

BUTTER

MILK

MUSTARD

FLOUR

CREAM

POTATO STARCH

TUSCAN BREAD (Unsalted)

SLICED BREAD

CURRY POWDER

BREAD CRUMBS

BALSAMIC VINEGAR

PICKLED ONIONS

OLIVES

PICKLED GHERKINS

EXTRA-VIRGIN OLIVE OIL

WHITE WINE

CAPERS (packed in salt)

COGNAC

RED WINE

BRANDY

EGGS

TUNA

TOMATO PASTE

ANCHOVY PASTE

ANCHOVIES

VEGETABLES

Vegetables and meat go together very well. Many of the recipes to follow include one or more vegetables in the basic ingredients. Most are quite common and can be found throughout the world in most seasons of the year. Finding fresh porcini mushrooms can be a problem, even in Italy. In most cases it is possible to substitute fresh porcini with an equal quantity of cultivated mushrooms combined with a small amount of dried and soaked porcini. The deep, woody aroma of the porcini is strong enough to penetrate the entire dish.

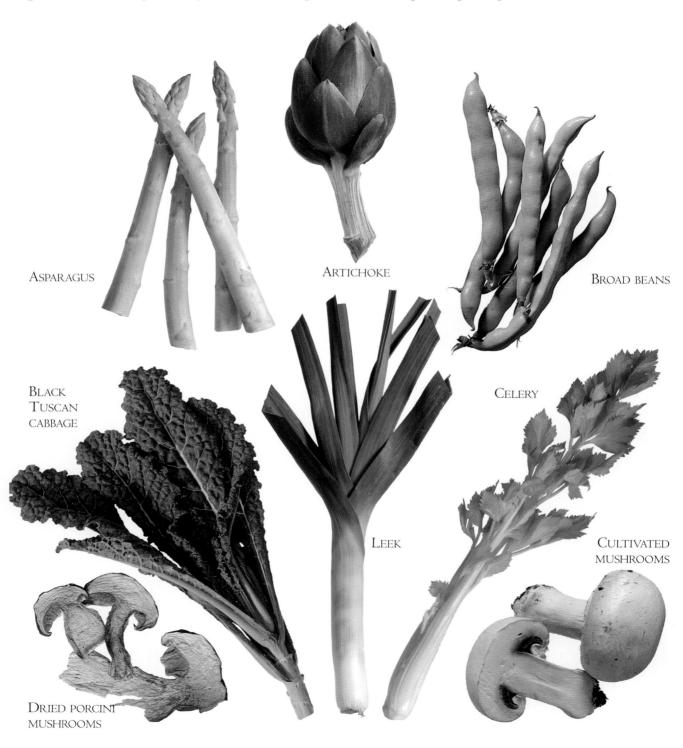

ASPARAGUS

ARTICHOKE

BROAD BEANS

BLACK TUSCAN CABBAGE

CELERY

LEEK

CULTIVATED MUSHROOMS

DRIED PORCINI MUSHROOMS

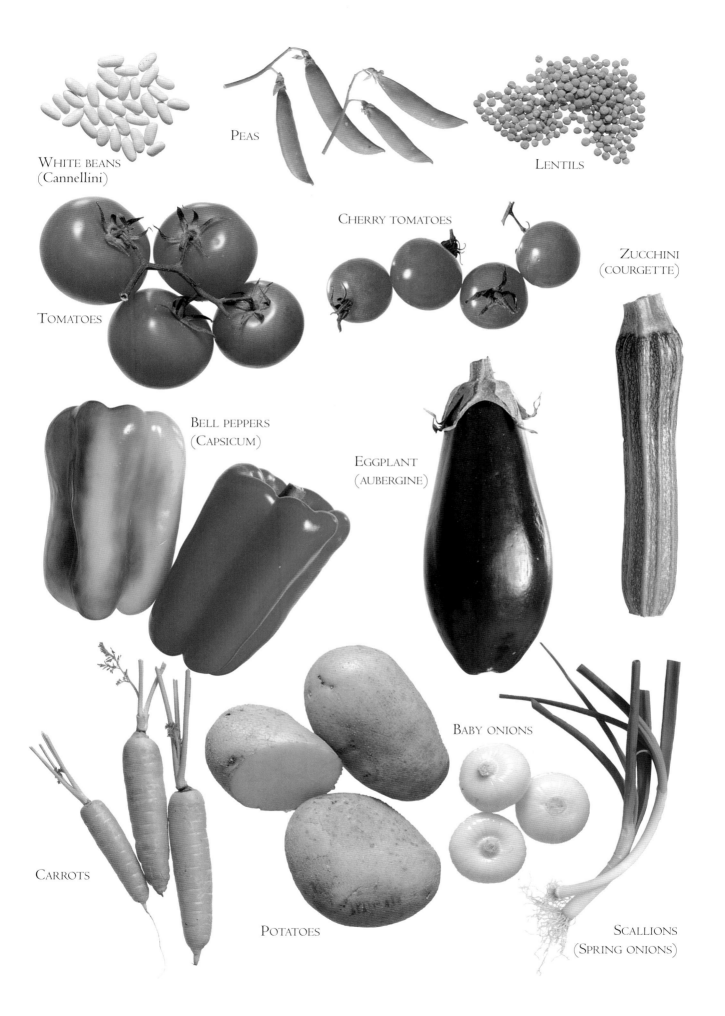

White beans
(Cannellini)

Peas

Lentils

Cherry tomatoes

Zucchini
(courgette)

Tomatoes

Bell peppers
(Capsicum)

Eggplant
(aubergine)

Baby onions

Carrots

Potatoes

Scallions
(Spring onions)

HERBS AND SPICES

Fresh herbs and freshly ground spices are essential ingredients in most Italian meat dishes. Common herbs, such as rosemary and sage, are so widely used that they are given free to good customers in most markets or vegetable stores without even being asked for. The herbs and spices on this page will all be easy to find in any good market or store. If possible, always use garden-fresh herbs and newly ground spices.

FENNEL

THYME

CALAMINT

TARRAGON

OREGANO

SAGE

FLAT-LEAF
PARSLEY

ARUGULA
(ROCKET)

BASIL

BAY LEAVES

FENNEL SEEDS

GARLIC

MIXED PEPPERCORNS

CHILIES

JUNIPER BERRIES

ROSEMARY

TRUFFLE

CLOVES

NUTMEG

RED, WHITE, AND GOLDEN ONIONS

SHALLOTS

FRUIT AND NUTS

The natural sweetness of fresh and dried fruit combines well with many meats. In recent years Italian cuisine has adopted (and adapted) recipes that use fruit from North Africa and many other parts of the world. I have included one or two of these "modern classics" here. But many recipes from the traditional repertoire also make use of fruit. Mustard sauce (see page 20) has been served with boiled and roast meats in northern Italy for centuries. Although duck served with orange (see p. 114) is now known as a French dish, it was originally taken to France by the Tuscan noblewoman, Catherine dei Medici, when she married the future king of France, Henry II, in the 16th century.

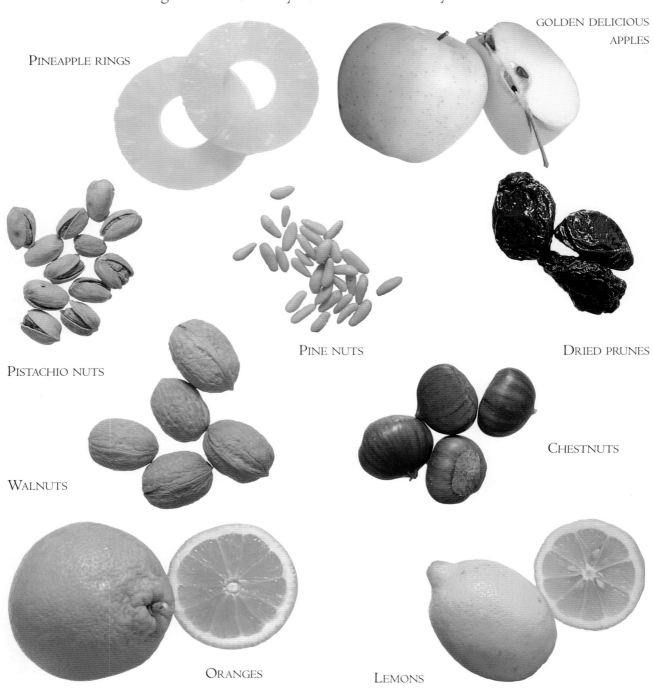

PINEAPPLE RINGS

GOLDEN DELICIOUS
APPLES

PISTACHIO NUTS

PINE NUTS

DRIED PRUNES

WALNUTS

CHESTNUTS

ORANGES

LEMONS

PREPARING AND COOKING MEAT

The many different cuts of meat can be cooked in a variety of ways. These are the most common cooking methods used in this book. I have also included a note on buying and preparing scaloppine and carpaccio, two cuts which may not be readily available at your local butcher or supermarket.

Brasato: braised meat is usually marinated before cooking to make it more tender and tastier. The marinade might consist of finely chopped carrots, celery, whole pepper grains, bay leaves, salt, and wine. The meat can be cooked with the same vegetables or fresh ones. Braising calls for long, slow cooking over low heat. The cooking juices are normally served with the meat.

Carpaccio: carpaccio is very thinly sliced top quality beef, usually fillet. Because it is eaten raw, the meat must be very good and very fresh.

Bollito: boiled meats are cooked in tall, narrow pans. The meat is generally immersed in cold water with vegetables, mixed aromatic herbs (usually carrots, onions, celery, and parsley), salt, and black pepper. Boiled meats are served either hot or at room temperature, depending on the season.

Fritto: for fried dishes, slice the meat thinly or chop in small pieces, dip it into beaten egg, and then dredge in bread crumbs or flour. Fry in very hot (but not smoking) olive oil until crisp and golden brown. Drain well on paper towels and serve very hot.

Stufato: when stewing meats, add all the ingredients (vegetables, herbs, meat, and liquid) to a heavy-bottomed pan at the same time. The dish is cooked slowly over low heat, usually for quite long periods of time.

Scaloppine: scaloppine are thin slices of veal cut from a single, solid piece of top round (topside). It is very important that the veal is sliced across the grain of the meat, otherwise the scaloppine will become tough during cooking. The meat should be cut in slices about ¼ in (6 mm) thick and lightly pounded before cooking.

Grigliata: barbecuing, grilling, or broiling all come in under this term. Barbecued meat can be marinated in oil, aromatic herbs, and lemon juice for an hour or two before cooking. Place the meat over glowing coals or embers, not flames, or it will burn on the outside and remain raw inside. Grilling meat indoors in a grill pan can also produce excellent results; prepare the meat as above, then place it in the grill pan. The grill pan should be very hot when the meat is added; when the meat has formed a thin crust, lower the heat to medium and cook until tender. Meat can also be broiled under an electric or gas coil. Prepare the meat as above and place under the preheated broiler.

Arrosto: oven-roasted meats should be sprinkled with a little salt and pepper and drizzled with oil before being placed in a preheated oven. Many recipes call for aromatic herbs, such as rosemary and sage, to be sprinkled over the roast before it goes into the oven.

Pan-roasting is another, more traditional way of preparing roast meat. The roast, prepared as above, should be placed in a heavy-bottomed pan over a burner at medium heat. The secret lies in leaving the pan partially covered and keeping just enough liquid (usually beef stock) in the bottom so that the roast does not stick. Be careful not to add too much liquid at once, because this will spoil the roast.

PORK PRODUCTS AND CHEESE

Cheese and pork products, such as ham, prosciutto, and sausages, are used to add extra flavor in many of the recipes. Although these are typically Italian products, most are now readily available in supermarkets and specialty stores. However, if you can't find prosciutto, provola, or any of the others, don't be afraid to substitute them with local ham (or bacon) and cheeses.

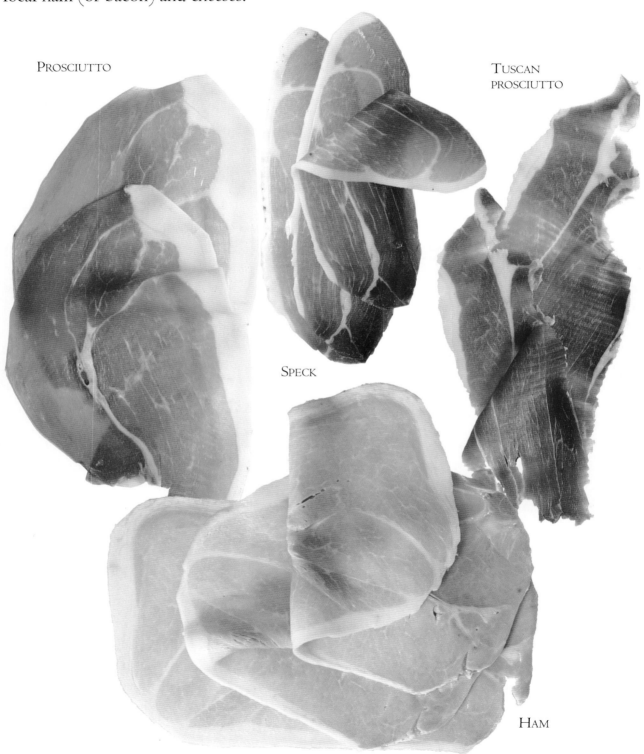

PROSCIUTTO

TUSCAN PROSCIUTTO

SPECK

HAM

PARMESAN
CHEESE

FONTINA
CHEESE

ITALIAN PORK
SAUSAGES

LARD

PANCETTA

MOZZARELLA
CHEESE

PROVOLA
CHEESE

MORTADELLA

Salsa di pomodoro
Simple tomato sauce

This delicious sauce will enhance any recipe that calls for fresh, ripe tomatoes (Scaloppine with pizza topping, Wild boar, Meatloaf, etc.). This recipe makes quite a large quantity; to keep in the refrigerator for 4-5 days, place in a jar or container and cover with a light film of oil before screwing on the lid.

Serves: 6-8; Preparation: 5 minutes; Cooking: 30 minutes; Level of difficulty: Simple

Combine the tomatoes and their liquid, onion, garlic, and parsley in a heavy-bottomed saucepan. § Bring to a boil over high heat, then lower the heat and partially cover with a lid. Simmer for 25 minutes, checking occasionally that there is enough liquid. If the sauce reduces too much during cooking, add a little water. § Press the sauce through a sieve or pass it through a food mill. § Add the salt, pepper, and basil, and return to heat to simmer for 5 more minutes. § Add the oil just before removing from heat. The uncooked oil will add its own special flavor to the sauce.

■ INGREDIENTS

- 3 cups (1½ lb/750 g) peeled and chopped fresh or canned tomatoes
- 2 onions, finely chopped
- 2 cloves garlic, finely chopped
- 3 tablespoons parsley, finely chopped
- salt and freshly ground black pepper
- 10 leaves fresh basil, torn
- 4 tablespoons extra-virgin olive oil

Salsa piccante al pomodoro
Hot tomato sauce

This versatile sauce is particularly good with mixed boiled, braised, or grilled meats.

Serves: 8-10; Preparation: 5 minutes; Cooking: 1 hour; Level of difficulty: Simple

Heat the oil in a small, heavy-bottomed pan over low heat. § Add the garlic and tomatoes. Sprinkle with salt, add the chilies and cook, partially covered, for at least an hour. § Serve hot or at room temperature.

■ INGREDIENTS

- 6 tablespoons extra-virgin olive oil
- 10 whole cloves garlic
- 2 cups (1 lb/500 g) peeled and chopped fresh or canned tomatoes
- salt
- 2 small hot chilies, dried or fresh, crumbled or sliced

Salsa acciugata
Anchovy sauce

This sauce is particularly good with fried lamb chops. It also makes an excellent pasta sauce.

Serves: 4; Preparation: 10 minutes; Cooking: 5 minutes; Level of difficulty: Simple

Rinse the anchovies thoroughly to remove extra salt. § Place the anchovies in a heavy-bottomed pan over medium-low heat. Mash well with a fork. Add the butter and cook, mixing frequently until creamy. § Serve hot.

■ INGREDIENTS

- 10 salted anchovy fillets, crumbled
- ⅔ cup (5 oz/150 g) butter

VARIATION
– Replace the anchovy fillets with 4 tablespoons of anchovy paste.

Right:
Salsa piccante al pomodoro

Salsa tartara
Tartare sauce

This sauce is excellent with boiled meats and fish.

Serves: 6; Preparation: 25 minutes; Level of difficulty: Simple

Prepare the mayonnaise. Be sure to use white vinegar instead of lemon juice in the mayonnaise when preparing Tartare sauce, because it goes better with the pickled ingredients. § Chop the pickled gherkins, onions, and capers finely and carefully mix with the mayonnaise. Stir in the mustard and serve.

■ INGREDIENTS

- 1 quantity *Mayonnaise*, made with vinegar (see recipe below)
- 2 pickled gherkins
- 2 pickled white onions
- 1 tablespoon capers in vinegar
- 1 teaspoon hot mustard

Salsa agliata
Garlic mayonnaise

This tasty sauce is perfect with all boiled meats and with many roast or braised ones too.

Serves: 4; Preparation: 15-20 minutes; Level of difficulty: Medium

Prepare the mayonnaise. Be sure to use lemon juice instead of white vinegar because it goes better with the garlic. § When the mayonnaise is ready, stir in the garlic, oil and pepper. Leave to stand for at least 1 hour before serving.

■ INGREDIENTS

- 1 quantity *Mayonnaise*, made with lemon juice (see recipe below)
- 2 cloves garlic, very finely chopped
- 1 tablespoon extra-virgin olive oil
- freshly ground black pepper

Salsa maionese
Mayonnaise

Making mayonnaise is not easy at first, but with a little patience you will master the art. The best results are achieved by hand, but I have also included instructions for making it in a blender.

Serves: 4; Preparation: 15-20 minutes; Level of difficulty: Medium

BY HAND: use a fork, wooden spoon or hand whisk to beat the egg yolk in a bowl with the salt. § Add the oil a drop at a time at first, then in a steady drizzle, stirring all the time in the same direction. § When the mayonnaise begins to thicken, add, very gradually, the lemon juice (or vinegar), the pepper and a few more drops of oil until it is the right density. § If the mayonnaise curdles, start over again with another egg yolk and use the curdled mayonnaise in place of the oil.

IN BLENDER: use the same ingredients as above, except for the egg, which should be whole. § Place the egg, salt, pepper, 1–2 tablespoons of oil and the lemon juice (or vinegar) in the blender and blend for a few seconds at maximum speed. § When the ingredients are well mixed, pour the remaining oil into the mixture very gradually. Continue blending until the right density is reached.

■ INGREDIENTS

- 1 fresh egg yolk
- salt
- ⅔ cup (5 fl oz/150 ml) extra-virgin olive oil
- 1 tablespoon lemon juice or white vinegar
- freshly ground black pepper

Right: Salsa tartara

Salsa mostarda
Mustard sauce

This sauce is typical of many regions of northern Italy where it is served with mixed, boiled meats. It also goes well with roast meats. The most famous version comes from Cremona. Leftover mustard sauce can be stored in sealed jars.

Serves: 12 (or more); Preparation: 15 minutes; Cooking: about 1 hour; Level of difficulty: Medium

Wash and peel the fruit. Cut into fairly large pieces, leaving the grapes and cherries whole. § Put the fruit in a heavy-bottomed saucepan and cover with water. Place over medium heat. Add the lemon juice and peel and 2 tablespoons of honey. § In a separate saucepan, simmer the wine with the remaining honey over medium-low heat. § After 10 minutes add the mustard to the wine and honey. Stir thoroughly and cook until thick. § Pour the mustard and wine mixture over the fruit and mix carefully. § Serve at room temperature.

■ INGREDIENTS

• 2 lb (1 kg) mixed fruit (white grapes, apples, pears, apricots, cherries, etc.)
• 1 lemon, juice and peel
• ½ cup (5 oz/150 g) liquid honey
• 1¾ cups (13 fl oz/ 400 ml) dry white wine
• 6 tablespoons mustard powder

Salsa alle cipolle
Onion sauce

This sauce is very simple to prepare, but takes a long time to cook. Make a double quantity and freeze any that is leftover. Onion sauce goes well with boiled and roast meats, and makes an excellent pasta sauce.

Serves: 6; Preparation: 15 minutes; Cooking: 3 hours; Level of difficulty: Simple

Place the onions in a heavy-bottomed pan with the oil over low heat. § Season with a little salt (use less than you normally would because the very slow cooking enhances the taste of the salt). Add a grinding of pepper and cover. § Cook gently over low heat for at least 3 hours. The onions must not burn, but should slowly melt. Stir frequently, adding stock, if necessary, to keep the sauce moist. § When cooked, the sauce should be creamy and golden.

■ INGREDIENTS

• 4 white onions, very thinly sliced
• 5 tablespoons extra-virgin olive oil
• salt and freshly ground black pepper
• ¾ cup (6 fl oz/180 ml) *Beef stock (see recipe p. 22)*

Right:
Salsa mostarda

SALSA VERDE
Parsley sauce with capers, anchovies, garlic, and oil

This sauce is traditionally served with boiled meats of all kinds.
It is excellent with thinly sliced, fried or braised meats as well.

Serves 4; Preparation: 15 minutes; Level of difficulty: Simple

Place all the ingredients in a food processor and blend. If 5 tablespoons of oil are not enough to make the sauce liquid, add more. Salt should not be necessary because of salt in the anchovies. § Serve at room temperature.

> VARIATIONS
> – Chop the white of a hard-cooked (hard boiled) egg and add to the sauce. If you wish, you can also add the yolk.
> – If you have the time, chop the ingredients by hand on a chopping board using a *mezzaluna* (a traditional semicircular chopper). The results will be well worth the effort.

■ INGREDIENTS

- 1 large bunch fresh parsley (leaves only), washed and dried
- 2 tablespoons capers
- 2 anchovy fillets
- 1 clove garlic
- 1 heaped teaspoon soft part of bread soaked in vinegar and squeezed thoroughly
- 5 tablespoons extra-virgin olive oil

BRODO DI CARNE
Beef stock

Beef stock is used in many of the recipes in this book. It helps to keep the ingredients moist during cooking and enriches the overall taste. Remember that stock will only keep in the refrigerator for about 3 days, although it freezes well. Freeze in small quantities and use as needed. If you are pushed for time and right out of frozen stock, beef stock made with a meat bouillon cube and boiling water can be used in any of the recipes calling for stock.

Makes: about 3 pints (1.5 liters); Preparation: 10 minutes; Cooking: 1½ hours; Level of difficulty: Simple

Put the meat, parsley, and vegetables in a large pot. Cover with 6½ pints (3 liters) of cold water and place over medium heat. § Reduce the heat when the water starts to boil. Move the lid so that the pot is partially covered and leave to simmer gently for at least an hour. § Remove the meat. Sprinkle the stock with the salt and leave to stand for 10 minutes. § Strain the vegetables and either mash with a fork and return to the stock or serve separately. § When the stock cools, the fat will harden on the top. Skim off and discard.

■ INGREDIENTS

- 1¼ lb (600 g) beef with bones (neck, shoulder, short ribs, brisket, various cuts of lean beef)
- 1 sprig parsley, whole with stalk
- 1 large carrot, cut in 2—3 pieces
- 1 large stalk celery, cut in 2—3 pieces
- 1 medium carrot, cut in half
- 6 small whole tomatoes, lightly cut on the surface
- ½ tablespoon coarse salt

Right:
Salsa verde

Turkey and Chicken

Turkey and chicken are readily available in Italy.
Both meats are reasonably cheap and are used in a
wide variety of dishes.

Pollo alla cacciatora
Braised chicken with tomato sauce and green olives

Serves: 4-6; Preparation: 15 minutes + 4 hours marinating; Cooking: 1 hour; Level of difficulty: Simple

Wash the chicken pieces under cold running water and pat dry with paper towels. § Place the chicken in a bowl and cover with 3 tablespoons of oil, the lemon juice, salt, and a generous grinding of pepper. Set aside to marinate for at least 4 hours. § Sauté the onion, carrot, and celery in the remaining oil over medium-high heat until the onion is soft. § Add the chicken pieces and sauté until golden. § Pour in the wine and cook until it evaporates, stirring frequently. § Add the tomatoes and water. Cover the sauté pan, lower the heat to medium, and continue to cook, stirring frequently. § After 15 minutes add the olives. Simmer gently over low heat for another 20 minutes, or until the chicken is tender. § Serve hot with green beans braised in tomatoes, or cooked spinach or Swiss chard sautéed briefly in garlic and oil.

VARIATIONS
– Replace the green olives with the same quantity of black olives.
– Replace the chicken with the same quantity of rabbit and cook as above.

INGREDIENTS

- 1 chicken, about 3 lb (1.5 kg) cut in 6–8 pieces
- 4 tablespoons extra-virgin olive oil
- juice of 1 lemon
- salt and freshly ground black pepper
- 1 onion, coarsely chopped
- 1 carrot, coarsely chopped
- 1 stalk celery, coarsely chopped
- ½ cup (4 fl oz/125 ml) dry white wine
- 1 lb (500 g) tomatoes, peeled and chopped
- ½ cup (4 fl oz/125 ml) cold water
- 1¼ cups (5 oz /150 g) green olives

Wine: a dry red (Piave Merlot or Corvo Rosso)

Polpettone avvolto nella verza
Turkey loaf wrapped in Savoy cabbage

Serves: 4-6; Preparation: 20 minutes; Cooking: 1¼ hours; Level of difficulty: Medium

Combine the turkey, sausage, pancetta, Parmesan, eggs, bread, nutmeg, salt, and pepper in a large bowl and mix thoroughly. Set aside. § Parboil the cabbage leaves in plenty of salted water for 4–5 minutes. Drain well and carefully pat dry with paper towels. § Arrange the cabbage leaves on a work surface to form a rectangle; they should be overlapping so that there is no space between the leaves. § Place the turkey mixture in the middle of the rectangle and shape into a meat loaf. § Wrap the cabbage leaves around the turkey loaf, taking care not to tear the leaves. Tie with a few twists of kitchen string. § Transfer the turkey loaf to an ovenproof dish with the shallots, tomatoes, and oil. § Bake in a

INGREDIENTS

- 1 lb (500 g) ground turkey breast
- 5 oz (150 g) Italian pork sausage, peeled and crumbled
- ½ cup (2 oz/60 g) pancetta, finely chopped
- ½ cup (2 oz/60 g) Parmesan cheese, freshly grated
- 1 egg + 1 yolk
- 2 tablespoons crustless bread, soaked in hot milk and well squeezed
- dash of nutmeg

Right: Pollo alla cacciatora

- salt and pepper
- 8–10 leaves Savoy cabbage
- 2 shallots, sliced
- 10 oz (300 g) tomatoes, peeled and chopped
- ⅓ cup (3½ fl oz/100 ml) extra-virgin olive oil
- ½ cup (4 fl oz/125 ml) dry white wine
- ½ cup (4 fl oz/125 ml) *Beef stock* (see recipe p. 22)

Wine: a dry rosé
(Rosato dei Colli Piacentini)

preheated oven at 400°F/200°C/gas 6 for 1¼ hours, basting frequently with the wine. When all the wine has been added, continue basting with the stock. § Slice the turkey loaf when lukewarm and serve.

VARIATION
— The turkey loaf can be cooked on the stove top over medium heat for 1½ hours instead of in the oven.

■ INGREDIENTS

- 2½ lb (1.2 kg) turkey breast
- 1 tablespoon mixed, chopped sage, rosemary, and garlic
- salt and freshly ground black pepper
- 10 oz (300 g) pancetta, sliced
- 4 tablespoons extra-virgin olive oil
- 1 lb (500 g) white baby onions, peeled
- 10 oz (300 g) carrots, peeled and sliced
- 1 lb (500 g) new potatoes, scraped
- ¾ cups (7 fl oz/200 ml) dry white wine
- 2 cups (16 fl oz/500 ml) *Beef stock* (see recipe p. 22)

Wine: a dry red (Rosso di Gallura)

■ INGREDIENTS

- 1 chicken, about 3 lb (1.5 kg) cut into 6–8 pieces
- 2 tablespoons butter
- 2 tablespoons extra-virgin olive oil
- salt and freshly ground black pepper
- dash of nutmeg
- ½ cup (4 fl oz/125 ml) dry white wine
- 1 tablespoon flour
- ¾ cup (7 fl oz/200 ml) *Beef stock* (see recipe p. 22)
- juice of ½ lemon

Wine: a dry white (Vespaiolo di Breganze)

Left:
Fesa di tacchino bardata alla pancetta

FESA DI TACCHINO BARDATA ALLA PANCETTA
Turkey breast wrapped in pancetta

Serves: 4-6; Preparation: 30 minutes; Cooking: 1 hour; Level of difficulty: Medium

Use a sharp knife to open the turkey breast out to a rectangular shape. Beat lightly with a meat pounder, taking care not to tear the meat. § Sprinkle with the herb mixture, salt, and pepper. § Roll the meat up and sprinkle with a little more salt and pepper. § Wrap the rolled turkey in the slices of pancetta so that it is completely covered and tie with kitchen string. § Transfer to a heavy-bottomed saucepan and add the oil. Sauté over high heat, turning all the time, until the meat is evenly browned. § After about 10 minutes, add the onions, carrots, and potatoes. § Add the wine, reduce the heat, cover, and cook for about 50 minutes more, stirring from time to time. Add stock as required during cooking to keep the meat moist — the bottom of the pan should always be covered with liquid. § When cooked, untie the turkey, slice (not too thinly), and arrange on a serving dish with the vegetables. § Serve hot with the cooking juices passed separately.

POLLO ALLA MARENGO
Marengo chicken

Napoleon Bonaparte's cook is said to have improvised this dish on the eve of the Battle of Marengo. The French General won a narrow victory over the Austrians on the Marengo Plain in northern Italy on June 4, 1800. Napoleon remained fond of the dish to the end of his days.

Serves: 4-6; Preparation: 15 minutes; Cooking: 1 hour; Level of difficulty: Simple

Wash the chicken under cold running water and pat dry with paper towels. § Transfer to a heavy-bottomed pan with the butter and oil and sauté until lightly browned. Season with salt, pepper, and nutmeg. § Discard most of the liquid that may have formed in the pan, add the wine, and stir in the flour. § Cook over medium-low heat for about 50 minutes, or until the chicken is tender. Add the stock as required during cooking to keep the chicken moist. § Arrange the chicken on a serving dish and drizzle with the lemon juice. § Serve hot with globe artichokes slowly braised in oil, garlic, and parsley.

Pollo arrosto
Italian-style roast chicken

■ INGREDIENTS

- 1 chicken, about 2½ lb (1.2 kg)
- 1 tablespoon fresh sage, finely chopped
- 1 tablespoon fresh rosemary, finely chopped
- 2 cloves garlic, finely chopped
- salt and freshly ground black pepper
- 1 lemon
- 4 tablespoons extra-virgin olive oil

Wine: a dry red (Chianti Classico)

Serves: 4; Preparation: 10 minutes; Cooking: 1 hour; Level of difficulty: Simple

Wash the chicken under cold running water and pat dry with paper towels. § Combine the sage, rosemary, garlic, salt, and pepper in a bowl. Mix well, then use to season the chicken inside and out. § Wash the lemon thoroughly, prick well with a fork and insert in the abdominal cavity of the chicken. This will make the meat tastier and absorb fat. § Place the chicken in a roasting pan greased with the oil. Bake in a preheated oven at 400°F/200°C/gas 6 for about 1 hour. § Turn the chicken every 15 minutes and baste with the oil and cooking juices. When cooked, the chicken should be very tender and the meat should come off the bone easily. The skin should be crisp. § Transfer to a heated serving dish. § Serve with roast or fried potatoes and a green salad.

Pollo novello al sale grosso
Spring chicken cooked in coarse salt

■ INGREDIENTS

- 9 lb (4½ kg) coarse salt
- 3 sprigs fresh sage
- 3 sprigs fresh rosemary
- 1 clove garlic, whole
- 1 chicken, about 2½ lb (1.2 kg)

Wine: a dry red (Rosso Conero)

Cooking meat or fish in salt enhances its taste. A crisp, salty crust forms on the outside, which can be nibbled on or discarded, as preferred, while the inside stays moist and tender. Surprisingly, in view of the cooking method, the meat is not at all salty.

Serves: 4; Preparation: 5 minutes; Cooking: 1½ hours; Level of difficulty: Simple

Spread 3 lb (1.5 kg) of coarse salt on the bottom of a high-sided baking dish. § Tie the herbs together and insert in the abdominal cavity of the chicken with the garlic. § Place the chicken in the baking dish and cover with the rest of the salt. No parts of the chicken should be visible. § Bake in a preheated oven at 375°F/190°C/gas 5 for 1½ hours. § Take out of the oven and remove the salt and herbs. Transfer to a heated serving dish. § Serve hot with baked potatoes and a green salad.

Right:
Pollo novello al sale grosso

GALANTINA DI POLLO
Chicken galantine (cold stuffed chicken)

This delicate dish is often served at Christmas time. It can be prepared well in advance and will keep for up to a week in the refrigerator. Serve thinly sliced as an appetizer or with a green or mixed salad as a light lunch or main course.

Serves: 8; Preparation: 40 minutes + 12 hours in refrigerator; Cooking: 1½ hours; Level of difficulty: Medium

Combine the beef, pork, turkey, veal, and mortadella in a large bowl. Mix well and add the pistachios, egg, and truffle. Sprinkle with salt and pepper and mix thoroughly. § Stuff the chicken with the mixture and sew up the neck and stomach cavity openings with a trussing needle and string. § Use your hands to give it a rectangular shape. Wrap in a piece of cheesecloth (muslin) and tie with kitchen string. § Place a large saucepan of salted water over medium heat. Add the onion, carrot, celery, parsley, peppercorns, and stock cube. § When the water is boiling, carefully add the stuffed chicken and simmer over low heat for 1½ hours. § Remove from the heat and drain the stock (which makes an excellent, light soup). § Remove the cheesecloth and place the chicken between two trays, with a weight (for example, a brick) on top. This will help to eliminate any liquid absorbed by the meat during cooking and will give it a rectangular shape. § When cool transfer to the refrigerator, with the weight still on top, and leave for at least 12 hours. § In the meantime prepare the gelatin, following the directions on the package. Be sure to add the lemon juice while the gelatin is still liquid. § Serve the galantine thinly sliced on a serving dish, topped with the diced gelatin.

■ INGREDIENTS

- 11 oz (325 g) lean ground beef
- 5 oz (150 g) lean ground pork
- 5 oz (150 g) ground turkey breast
- 5 oz (150 g) ground suckling veal
- 2 oz (60 g) ground mortadella
- ½ cup (2½ oz / 75 g) pistachios, shelled
- 1 egg
- 1 oz (30 g) black truffle, finely sliced (optional)
- salt and freshly ground black pepper
- 1 chicken, boneless, about 4 lb (2 kg)
- 1 onion, cut in half
- 1 carrot, cut in 3
- 1 stalk celery, cut in 3
- 2 sprigs parsley
- 7–8 peppercorns
- 1 chicken stock cube
- 2 gelatin cubes
- juice of ½ lemon

Wine: a light, dry white (Soave Classico)

VARIATION
– Make the chicken galantine without the truffle. It will certainly be cheaper to make, though with the truffle it is another dish entirely!

Right:
Galantina di pollo

Filetti di pollo alla crema di formaggio
Chicken breast with cheese sauce

■ INGREDIENTS

- 1 lb (500 g) chicken breast, sliced in fillets
- 4 tablespoons extra-virgin olive oil
- salt and black pepper
- 4 oz (125 g) Fontina cheese, sliced
- ¼ cup (2 oz/60 g) chopped ham (optional)
- ¾ cup (7 fl oz/200 ml) whole milk

Wine: a dry white (Cirò Bianco)

Serves: 4; Preparation: 10 minutes; Cooking: 20 minutes; Level of difficulty: Simple

Place the fillets of chicken in a large sauté pan with the oil over medium heat and sauté until golden brown on both sides. Season with salt and pepper. § Cover each fillet with slices of cheese and a sprinkling of ham, if using. Carefully pour the milk over the top. § Continue cooking until the cheese has melted and the milk has reduced to a creamy sauce. § Serve hot with a side dish of baked fennel (lightly boiled fennel in béchamel sauce sprinkled with Parmesan cheese and baked in a hot oven).

Insalata di pollo e peperoni sott'olio
Chicken and bell pepper salad

This delicious salad is easy to prepare.
It makes an ideal appetizer or light lunch.

Serves: 4; Preparation: 20 minutes + 1 hour for the chicken; Cooking: 1 hour; Level of difficulty: Simple

Boil the chicken in a large pot of water with the carrot, onion, celery, parsley, and salt for about 1 hour. When cooked, drain and set aside to cool. § Remove the skin and bones and cut the chicken into small pieces. Transfer to a salad bowl. § Drain the bell peppers from the oil and coarsely chop. Add to the chicken together with the pine nuts and arugula. § Season with salt, pepper, oil, and vinegar just before serving. Toss well.

■ INGREDIENTS

• 1 chicken, about 2 lb (1 kg)
• 1 carrot, 1 onion, 1 stalk celery, cut in half
• small bunch parsley
• salt and freshly ground black pepper
• 4 oz (125 g) red bell peppers (capsicums) in oil
• ½ cup (3½ oz/100 g) pine nuts
• 2 bunches arugula (rocket), coarsely chopped
• 4 tablespoons extra-virgin olive oil
• 2 tablespoons white vinegar

Wine: a dry, sparkling white (Prosecco di Valdobbiadene)

Fesa di tacchino in crosta
Turkey breast pie

Serves: 4-6; Preparation: 45 minutes; Cooking: 1¼ hours; Level of difficulty: Medium

Use a sharp knife to open the turkey breast out to a rectangular shape. Beat lightly with a meat pounder, taking care not to tear the meat. § Sauté the zucchini, carrot, and onion in 2 tablespoons of butter until the onion is soft. Season with salt and pepper and set aside to cool for a few minutes. § Sprinkle the turkey with salt and pepper, cover with the ham, and scatter with the vegetables. § Roll the meat up and wrap with slices of pancetta. Truss with kitchen string, making two twists lengthwise as well, to fix the pancetta firmly to the turkey. § Place the meat in an ovenproof dish with the garlic, sage, and oil. Cook in a preheated oven at 400°F/200°C/gas 6 for 50 minutes, turning the meat over during cooking and basting with the wine from time to time. § Set the meat aside to cool. Discard the kitchen string; the meat will keep its shape when cool. § On a lightly floured work surface, roll the pastry out to a thin sheet. Wrap it round the meat, brush with the egg and decorate with pieces of leftover pastry. § Butter and flour a baking sheet and bake in a preheated oven at 400°F/200°C/gas 6 for 20 minutes. § Serve hot with a green or mixed salad.

■ INGREDIENTS

• 2½ lb (1.2 kg) turkey breast
• 1 zucchini (courgette) and 1 carrot, sliced in julienne strips
• 1 onion, thinly sliced
• 2½ tablespoons butter
• salt and freshly ground black pepper
• 4 oz (125 g) ham, sliced
• 7 oz (200 g) pancetta, thinly sliced
• 1 clove garlic, cut in half
• 4 leaves sage
• ⅓ cup (3½ fl oz/100 ml) extra-virgin olive oil
• ½ cup (4 fl oz/125 ml) dry white wine
• 10 oz (300 g) frozen puff pastry, thawed
• 1 egg, beaten

Wine: a dry white (Pinot Grigio)

Right: Fesa di tacchino in crosta

Polpettine di pollo ai peperoni e olive nere
Chicken balls with bell peppers and black olives

Serves: 6; Preparation: 40 minutes; Cooking: about 40 minutes; Level of difficulty: Medium

Cut the eggplant in thick slices, sprinkle with salt and place in a colander for about 20 minutes. Cut into cubes. § Heat 4 tablespoons of the oil in a large sauté pan over medium heat and sauté the garlic and onion until soft. § Add the peppers, eggplant, zucchini, tomatoes, and olives. Season with salt and pepper. Stir and cook for about 20 minutes, adding a little water if the pan becomes too dry. § In the meantime, combine the chicken, bread, Parmesan, egg, parsley, and a little salt in a bowl and mix thoroughly. § Shape the mixture (which should be quite firm) into small round balls, then coat with flour. § Heat the remaining oil in a large sauté pan over a medium heat and fry the balls until golden brown all over. § Add the vegetable mixture, season with salt and pepper, and cook for 15 minutes more, stirring carefully. If the dish dries out too much, add stock as required. § Transfer to a heated serving dish, sprinkle with the basil and serve hot.

Pollo ai funghi porcini
Chicken with porcini mushrooms

If you can't get porcini mushrooms, use the same quantity of white mushrooms mixed with 1½ tablespoons of dried porcini (soaked in warm water for 20 minutes, squeezed dry, and chopped).

Serves: 4-6; Preparation: 30 minutes; Cooking: about 1 hour; Level of difficulty: Medium

Wash and dry the chicken and cut into 8–10 pieces. § Clean the mushrooms, rinse and pat dry carefully with paper towels. Cut the stems into chunks, and the caps into fairly large strips. § Melt 1 tablespoon of butter in a heavy-bottomed pan over medium heat. Add 1 tablespoon of

■ INGREDIENTS

- 1 eggplant (aubergine)
- salt and freshly ground black pepper
- ½ cup (4 fl oz/125 ml) extra-virgin olive oil
- 1 clove garlic
- 1 large onion, thickly sliced
- 2 bell peppers (capsicums), red, yellow, or green, diced
- 1 zucchini (courgette), diced
- 10 cherry tomatoes, cut in half
- ½ cup(1¾ oz/50 g) black olives
- 1¼ lb (600 g) ground chicken breast
- 2 tablespoons crustless bread, soaked in milk and squeezed
- ½ cup (2 oz/60 g) Parmesan cheese, freshly grated
- 1 egg
- 1 tablespoon parsley, finely chopped
- ½ cup (2 oz/60 g) flour
- ½ cup (4 fl oz/125 ml) *Beef stock* (see recipe p. 22)
- 10 leaves basil, torn

Wine: a dry white (Verdicchio)

■ INGREDIENTS

- 1 chicken, about 2½ lb (1.2 kg)
- 1 lb (500 g) porcini mushrooms
- 2 tablespoons butter
- 3 tablespoons extra-virgin olive oil
- 1 clove garlic, finely chopped

Right: *Polpettine di pollo ai peperoni e olive nere*

- 2 sprigs mint
- salt and freshly ground black pepper
- 1 tablespoon parsley, finely chopped
- ½ cup (4 fl oz/125 ml) dry white wine
- 1 white onion, coarsely chopped
- ¾ cup (7 fl oz/200 ml) milk

Wine: a dry white
(Riesling Renano dei Colli Berici)

oil and sauté the garlic briefly. § Add the mushrooms and mint. Season with salt, and pepper and cook for a few minutes. Scatter with the parsley, remove from heat and set aside. § Place the remaining butter and oil in a sauté pan over medium heat. Add the chicken, salt, and pepper, and brown on all sides. § Pour in the wine and cook over high heat until it evaporates. § Add the onion and cook until soft. § Pour in the milk and reduce the heat. Add salt and pepper to taste, cover the pan and cook for 30 minutes more, stirring frequently. § Remove the lid; if the sauce is too liquid, raise the heat until it reduces a little. § Add the mushrooms, stir well, and cook over medium-low heat for 5 minutes more. § Transfer to a heated serving dish and serve hot.

Bocconcini di pollo al curry
Chicken pieces with curry

Serves: 4; Preparation: 15 minutes; Cooking: 25 minutes; Level of difficulty: Simple

Chop the chicken into bite-sized pieces, rinse under cold running water, and pat dry with paper towels. § Place the flour in a bowl and dredge the chicken pieces, shaking off excess flour. § Melt the butter in a skillet (frying pan) and sauté the onion over medium heat until soft. § Add the chicken, season with salt and pepper, and sauté for 2–3 minutes. § Pour in the cognac. When it has evaporated, add the cream and curry. § Continue cooking over low heat, partially covered, and stirring frequently for about 20 minutes, or until the sauce reduces. § Transfer to a heated serving dish. Serve hot with boiled spring carrots and new potatoes, or spring peas with parsley.

VARIATION
– Serve the chicken and vegetables on a bed of boiled white or brown rice for a nourishing one-course meal.

■ INGREDIENTS

- 2 lb (1 kg) chicken, boned
- 4 tablespoons flour
- 4 tablespoons butter
- 1 white onion, thinly sliced
- salt and freshly ground black pepper
- ½ cup (4 fl oz/125 ml) cognac (or brandy)
- ½ cup (4 fl oz/125 ml) fresh cream
- 1 teaspoon curry powder

Wine: a dry rosé (Cerveteri Rosato or Bardolino Chiaretto)

Fesa di tacchino alla crema di cipolle
Chicken breast in cream of onion sauce

Serves: 6; Preparation: 15 minutes; Cooking: 1¼ hours; Level of difficulty: Simple

Roll the turkey breast and tie with kitchen string. Season with salt and pepper and roll in the flour. § Transfer to a heavy-bottomed pan with the oil and butter and sauté over high heat for 5–7 minutes. § Add the onions, stirring carefully and making sure the turkey is always touching the bottom of the pan (rather than on the onions). Sauté for 5 minutes more. § Pour in enough stock to almost cover the meat. Partially cover the pan and lower the heat to medium. Add more stock during cooking, as required. § When cooked, the turkey will be light brown and the onions will have melted to form a delicious, creamy sauce. § Serve hot cut in ½-in (1-cm) thick slices or cold in thin slices. Arrange the slices on a serving dish and smother with the onion sauce. If serving cold, reheat the onion sauce just before serving. § Serve with hot potato purée.

VARIATION
– Replace the onions with 6–8 medium carrots cut in slices. Equally delicious, the sauce will be sweeter with a more delicate taste.

■ INGREDIENTS

- 2½ lb (1.2 kg) turkey breast
- salt and freshly ground black pepper
- 3 tablespoons flour
- ½ cup (4 fl oz/125 ml) extra-virgin olive oil
- 1 tablespoon butter
- 4 large white onions, coarsely sliced
- 4 cups (2 pints/1 liter) *Beef stock (see recipe p. 22)*

Wine: a dry red (Donnaz)

Right: *Fesa di tacchino alla crema di cipolle*

VEAL AND BEEF

Many of the most popular Italian meat dishes are made with veal or beef. These range from classics like Florentine steak, or Beef braised in red wine, to more refined dishes, such as Carpaccio and arugula, or Veal scaloppine in white wine.

Stracotto toscano
Tuscan-style braised beef

In this traditional Tuscan recipe, the beef is braised slowly in red wine and stock. After 3 hours the meat is extremely tender. If there is any braised beef leftover, chop the meat finely, mix with the sauce and serve the next day with fresh pasta, such as tagliatelle or tortelloni.

Serves: 4-6; Preparation: 25 minutes; Cooking: 3 hours; Level of difficulty: Medium

Mix the garlic and rosemary with a generous quantity of salt and pepper. Using a sharp knife, make several incisions in the meat and fill with the herb mixture. § Tie the meat loosely with kitchen string. § Heat the oil in a heavy-bottomed pan over medium-high heat and brown the meat well on all sides. § Add the onions, carrots, celery, parsley, sage, and bay leaves and sauté for a few minutes. § Season with salt and pepper, then pour in the wine. When the wine has evaporated, add the tomatoes, partially cover and simmer over medium-low heat for about 2½ hours. § Turn the meat from time to time, adding the stock gradually so that the sauce doesn't dry out. § When the meat is cooked, transfer to a heated serving dish and cut in slices. Spoon the sauce and cooking juices over the top, and serve hot.

> VARIATION
> – For an even tastier dish, wrap the meat in 3½ oz (100 g) of sliced pancetta (tied firmly with kitchen string) before cooking.

■ INGREDIENTS
- 1 clove garlic, finely chopped
- 1 tablespoon rosemary, finely chopped
- salt and freshly ground black pepper
- 2 lb (1 kg) beef (rump or sirloin)
- ⅓ cup (3½ fl oz/100 ml) extra-virgin olive oil
- 2 onions, coarsely chopped
- 2 carrots, coarsely chopped
- 1 stalk celery, coarsely chopped
- 1 tablespoon parsley, finely chopped
- 3 leaves sage, torn
- 2 bay leaves
- ¾ cup (7 fl oz/200 ml) dry red wine
- 14 oz (450 g) tomatoes, peeled and chopped
- 2 cups (16 fl oz/500 ml) Beef stock (see recipe p. 22)

Wine: a dry red (Chianti Classico)

Rognoncini trifolati alla salvia
Kidneys with oil, garlic, parsley, and sage

This tasty peasant dish is now served in top restaurants, where it passes for haute cuisine.

Serves: 4; Preparation: 15 minutes + 1 hour for the meat; Cooking: 8 minutes; Level of difficulty: Simple

Slice the kidneys in two lengthways, and remove the fatty parts and sinews. Cut into thin slices and set aside in a bowl of cold water and vinegar for about 1 hour. § Heat the oil and butter in a heavy-bottomed pan over medium-high heat. Add the garlic, parsley, and sage and sauté for 2–3 minutes. § Add the kidneys. Season with salt and pepper and pour in the wine. § Cook for 5 minutes only, or the kidneys will become tough. § Serve hot with potato purée and the cooking juices from the pan.

■ INGREDIENTS
- 1 lb (500 g) calf's kidneys
- ¾ cup (7 fl oz/200 ml) vinegar
- 4 tablespoons extra-virgin olive oil
- 1 tablespoon butter
- 2 cloves garlic, finely chopped
- 1 tablespoon parsley, finely chopped
- 5 sage leaves
- salt and black pepper
- ½ cup (4 fl oz/125 ml) red wine

Right: Stracotto toscano

Fetta di vitello alla valdostana
Aosta Valley-style veal slices

■ INGREDIENTS

- 1 lb (500 g) veal, cut from the rump, in a single slice
- salt and freshly ground black pepper
- 4 oz (125 g) sliced speck
- 4 oz (125 g) Fontina cheese, sliced
- 1 scant tablespoon oregano
- ⅓ cup (3½ fl oz/100 ml) extra-virgin olive oil
- ½ cup (4 fl oz/125 ml) dry white wine
- 1 cup (8 fl oz/250 ml) Beef stock (see recipe p. 22)

Wine: a dry red (Grignolino)

Serves: 4; Preparation: 15 minutes; Cooking: 1¼ hours; Level of difficulty: Simple

Remove any pieces of fat from the meat. Cover with foil and beat lightly with a meat pounder (the foil prevents the meat from breaking). § Sprinkle with salt and pepper. Cover with the speck and top with the Fontina. § Sprinkle with the oregano and roll up the meat. Tie with kitchen string and transfer to a heavy-bottomed pan. § Pour in the oil and place over a medium-high heat. Cook until brown on both sides. § Pour in the wine and reduce the heat. § When the wine has evaporated, partially cover and cook for about 1 hour, adding stock as the pan dries out, and turning the meat from time to time. § Transfer to a heated serving dish and smother with the cooking juices. § Serve with boiled broccoli sautéed in garlic, crushed chillies, and olive oil.

Straccetti alla rucola
Thinly sliced sirloin with arugula

■ INGREDIENTS

- 10 oz (300 g) sirloin, thinly sliced
- 2 bunches arugula (rocket)
- salt and freshly ground black pepper
- juice of ½ lemon
- 4 tablespoons extra-virgin olive oil

Wine: a dry, aromatic white (Müller Thurgau)

This light and healthy dish is always delicious, especially in summer.

Serves: 4; Preparation: 10 minutes; Cooking: 20 minutes; Level of difficulty: Simple

Wash and dry the arugula, cut finely, and set aside. § Heat a large nonstick sauté pan over medium-high heat. Cook the slices of beef, 2–3 at a time, by dropping them into the pan and turning them immediately. They will only take a minute or two to cook. § When all the beef is cooked, arrange the slices on a heated serving dish, sprinkle with salt and pepper, and cover with the arugula. Sprinkle lightly with salt and pepper again and drizzle with the oil and lemon juice. § Toss the arugula and serve immediately.

Left: Straccetti alla rucola

Saltimbocca alla romana
Veal slices with prosciutto and sage

Serves: 4; Preparation: 15 minutes; Cooking: 12 minutes; Level of difficulty: Simple

Pound the slices of meat and lightly flour. § Place ½ slice of prosciutto on each and top with a sage leaf. § Use a toothpick to fix the prosciutto and sage to the slice of veal. § Melt the butter and oil in a large sauté pan. Add the veal slices, with the prosciutto facing downward. Brown on both sides over high heat. § Season with salt and pepper (taste first, the prosciutto is already salty and you may not need much more). § Pour in the wine and cook for 5–6 minutes more. § Serve hot with a side dish of spinach or Swiss chard sautéed in butter.

■ INGREDIENTS

• 14 oz (450 g) veal, preferably rump, cut in 8 slices
• 4 oz (125 g) prosciutto
• 8 leaves sage
• 4 tablespoons flour
• 2 tablespoons butter
• 3 tablespoons extra-virgin olive oil
• salt and freshly ground black pepper
• ½ cup (4 fl oz/125 ml) dry white wine

*Wine: a dry red
(Chianti Classico)*

Bistecca alla fiorentina
Grilled T-bone steak, Florentine-style

For steak-lovers, a grilled Florentine T-bone steak is the ultimate treat. In Italy, the steak is cut from Chianina beef (a breed native to Tuscany) and hung for at least 6 days before cooking. For best results, the steak should be cooked over the embers of a charcoal or wood-burning grill. Florentines eat their steaks very rare; some claim that the meat inside, near the bone, should only just be warm! This is a matter of taste and you can increase the cooking time accordingly.

Serves: 2; Preparation: 3 minutes; Cooking: 10 minutes; Level of difficulty: Simple

Remove any sinews and excess fat from the meat. Season with a generous grinding of black pepper. § Place on a grill over very hot embers. After 5–6 minutes turn the steak using a wooden spatula (do not use a fork since the steak must not be pierced), and cook for another 5–6 minutes. The secret of this dish lies in the speed of cooking: the meat must be well roasted outside, but rare inside so that when it is cut the juices ooze out onto the plate. § Sprinkle with salt and serve straight from the grill. § Serve with grilled mushroom caps (preferably porcini) seasoned with thyme, sliced garlic, salt, and pepper.

■ INGREDIENTS

• 2 lb (1 kg) T-bone steak
• salt and freshly ground black pepper

*Wine: a dry red
(Brunello di Montalcino)*

Right:
Saltimbocca alla romana

Trippa alla fiorentina
Florentine-style tripe

*Tripe vendors can still be seen in the streets of Florence selling their tripe
sandwiches or containers with hot tripe (plastic nowadays, and served with plastic forks).
The mouth-watering aroma of tomato and tripe wafts through the streets and few real
Florentines can resist stopping off now and then for a bite to eat.*

Serves: 4-6; Preparation: 20 minutes; Cooking: 1 hour; Level of difficulty: Simple

Rinse the tripe, drain well, and cut into strips about ½ in (1 cm) wide
and 3 in (7.5 cm) long. § Sauté the onion, carrot, celery, and garlic in the
oil and butter in a heavy-bottomed pan, preferably made of earthenware.
§ When the vegetable mixture is pale gold, pour in the wine and cook
until it evaporates. § Add the tripe. The tripe will release water as it
cooks; cook until this has reduced and then add the tomatoes. § Season
with salt and pepper, stir well and add a ladleful of stock. § Cover and
continue cooking over low heat for about 1 hour. Stir frequently, adding
more stock if the tripe becomes too dry. § If the sauce is too liquid,
uncover the pan and increase the heat until the sauce reduces. § Serve
hot with the Parmesan and with a side dish of boiled white or red
kidney beans seasoned with oil, salt, and pepper.

■ INGREDIENTS

• 2 lb (1 kg) ready-to-cook
  honeycomb tripe,
  thawed, if frozen
• 1 medium onion, 1 carrot,
  1 stalk celery, 1 clove garlic,
  all finely chopped
• 4 tablespoons extra-virgin
  olive oil
• 3 tablespoons butter
• ½ cup (4 fl oz/125 ml)
  dry white wine
• 12 oz (350 g) tomatoes,
  peeled and chopped
• 2 cups (16 fl oz/500 ml)
  Beef stock (see recipe p. 22)
• salt and freshly ground
  black pepper
• 1 cup (4 oz/125 g)
  Parmesan cheese, freshly
  grated

*Wine: a dry red
(Rosso di Montalcino)*

Trippa alla milanese
Milanese-style tripe

Serves: 4; Preparation: 25 minutes; Cooking: 1 hour; Level of difficulty: Simple

Sauté the leek, carrot, and celery in the oil in a heavy-bottomed pan,
preferably made of earthenware. § When the vegetables are pale gold, add
the tripe and season with salt and pepper. § Stir again and add the shin
bone. § Partially cover and cook gently for about 1 hour in the liquid
produced by the tripe. Stir frequently, adding a little hot water if the
tripe dries out too much. § Sprinkle with the Parmesan and serve hot.

■ INGREDIENTS

• 1 leek, 1 carrot, 1 stalk
  celery, finely chopped
• 4 tablespoons extra-virgin
  olive oil
• 1¾ lb (800 g) ready-to-
  cook honeycomb tripe,
  thawed, if frozen
• salt and freshly ground
  black pepper
• 1 shin bone
• 1 cup (4 oz/125 g)
  Parmesan cheese, freshly
  grated

Wine: a dry white (Riesling)

Right: *Trippa alla fiorentina*

■ INGREDIENTS

- 2 medium onions, sliced
- 4 tablespoons extra-virgin olive oil
- 1¼ lb (600 g) calf's liver, cut in short, thin strips
- ½ cup (4 fl oz/125 ml) dry white wine
- ½ cup (4 fl oz/125 ml) white vinegar
- salt and freshly ground black pepper

Wine: a dry red (Raboso Veronese)

FEGATO ALLA VENEZIANA
Sautéed calf's liver, Venetian-style

Serves: 4; Preparation: 15 minutes; Cooking: 20-25 minutes; Level of difficulty: Simple

Sauté the onions in the oil over medium-low heat for about 10 minutes. § Add the liver, turn up the heat and stir rapidly. § Pour in the wine and vinegar and season with salt and pepper. Cook until the liquids have evaporated. § When the sauce is well-reduced, turn off the heat. § Serve hot with a side dish of potato purée.

VARIATION
— For a stronger tasting dish, use the darker liver of a full-grown animal.

Francesina ai porri
Boiled beef in leek and tomato sauce

This recipe provides a good way to use up the leftover beef when you have made beef stock. The boiled beef will keep in the refrigerator for 2 days, so you can make these the day after making stock.

Serves: 4; Preparation: 15 minutes; Cooking: 30 minutes; Level of difficulty: Simple

Cut the boiled beef into bite-sized pieces. § Heat the oil in a heavy-bottomed pan and sauté the leeks for a few minutes. § Pour in the stock and partially cover. Cook until the liquid has almost completely reduced. § Add the meat and tomatoes, season with salt and pepper, and continue cooking for about 20 minutes, or until the meat is literally falling apart. § Transfer to a serving dish and serve hot with potatoes or rice.

VARIATION
– The classic version of this recipe calls for the same quantity of thickly sliced white or red onions in place of the leeks. Scallions (spring onions) can also be used.

■ INGREDIENTS

- 1 lb (500 g) boiled beef (neck, shoulder, short ribs, brisket, various cuts of lean beef)
- 4 tablespoons extra-virgin olive oil
- 4 leeks, sliced
- ¾ cup (7 fl oz/200 ml) *Beef stock (see recipe p. 22)*
- 12 oz (350 g) tomatoes, peeled and chopped
- salt and freshly ground black pepper

Wine: a dry red (Barbera)

Brasato al barolo
Braised beef in a red wine sauce

Serves: 6; Preparation: 15 minutes + 24 hours to marinate; Cooking: 2¼ hours; Level of difficulty: Simple

Place the meat in a bowl with the onion, carrot, celery, bay leaves, and peppercorns. Cover with the wine and set aside to marinate for 24 hours. § Remove the meat from the marinade and pat dry with paper towels. Tie firmly with kitchen string. § Heat the oil and butter over medium heat in a heavy-bottomed saucepan just large enough to contain the meat. Add the meat, sprinkle with salt, and brown on all sides. § In the meantime, strain the wine from the marinade. Pour about half the wine over the meat, cover the pan and simmer gently for 2 hours, turning the meat from time to time. § The sauce should be quite thick when the meat is cooked. § Slice the meat and transfer to a heated serving dish. Pour the sauce over the top and serve hot with a side dish of potato purée.

■ INGREDIENTS

- 2½ lb (1.2 kg) boneless beef roast, preferably chuck
- 1 onion, sliced
- 1 carrot, sliced
- 1 stalk celery, sliced
- 2 bay leaves
- 1 teaspoon peppercorns
- 4 cups (2 pints/1 liter) Barolo wine (or another good, robust red wine)
- ⅓ cup (3½ fl oz/100 ml) extra-virgin olive oil
- 1 tablespoon butter
- salt

Wine: a dry red (Barolo)

Right: *Francesina ai porri*

Vitello al latte farcito
Veal roll with cheese and prosciutto filling

This versatile dish can be served with most boiled or braised vegetables, and salads.

Serves: 6; Preparation: 20 minutes; Cooking: about 1 hour; Level of difficulty: Medium

Remove any small pieces of fat from the meat. Cover with foil (to prevent the meat from breaking) and lightly pound. § Season with salt and pepper, cover with slices of prosciutto and Fontina, and sprinkle with Parmesan. § Roll the veal up tightly (with the grain of the meat running parallel to the length of the roll, so that it will be easier to slice) and tie firmly with kitchen string. § Heat the oil over medium-low heat in a heavy-bottomed saucepan just large enough to contain the roll. § Brown the roll on all sides and sprinkle with salt and pepper. § Pour in the milk (which should cover the roll), partially cover the saucepan, and continue cooking over medium heat until the milk reduces. This will take about 1 hour. Turn the meat from time to time during cooking. § Transfer to a serving dish, slice and serve hot or at room temperature. If serving cold, reheat the sauce, and pour over the sliced roll.

■ INGREDIENTS

- 1½ lb (750 g) slice of veal, preferably rump
- salt and freshly ground black pepper
- 4 oz (125 g) prosciutto
- 4 oz (125 g) Fontina cheese, sliced
- 4 oz (125 g) Parmesan cheese, in flakes
- 4 tablespoons extra-virgin olive oil
- 2 cups (16 fl oz/500 ml) milk

Wine: a dry white (Müller Thurgau)

Carré di vitello ai porri
Loin of veal with leeks

Serves: 6; Preparation: 20 minutes; Cooking: 1¼ hours; Level of difficulty: Medium

Tie the veal firmly with kitchen string. Season with salt and pepper. § Sauté the meat with the oil and butter in a heavy-bottomed saucepan just large enough to contain the veal. § When the meat is brown, add the leeks and cook for 5 minutes, stirring frequently. Season with salt and pepper. § Pour in the milk so that it covers the meat and cook for about 1 hour, or until the milk evaporates. § Remove the meat, slice and transfer to a heated serving dish. § Chop the sauce in a food processor or food mill and spoon it over the meat. § Serve hot with boiled peas and parsley.

■ INGREDIENTS

- 2½ lb (1.2 kg) veal loin
- salt and freshly ground black pepper
- ⅓ cup (3½ fl oz/100 ml) extra-virgin olive oil
- 2 tablespoons butter
- 3 leeks, sliced
- 4 cups (2 pints/1 liter) milk

Wine: a dry red (Chianti dei Colli Fiorentini)

VARIATION
– Replace the leeks with 2 large white onions.

Right:
Vitello al latte farcito

INGREDIENTS

- 1 onion, finely chopped
- 4 tablespoons extra-virgin olive oil
- 4 hamburgers made from 1 lb (500 g) lean beef
- salt and black pepper
- ½ cup (4 fl oz/125 ml) dry white wine
- ½ cup (4 fl oz/125 ml) *Beef stock* (see recipe p. 22)
- 4 teaspoons mustard

Wine: a dry red (Dolcetto d'Alba)

HAMBURGER ALLA SALSA DI SENAPE
Hamburgers in white wine and mustard sauce

Serves: 4; Preparation: 10 minutes; Cooking: 20 minutes; Level of difficulty: Simple

Sauté the onion in the oil in a heavy-bottomed pan over medium heat until soft. § Add the hamburgers and season with salt and pepper. Pour in the wine and cook until it evaporates, turning the hamburgers frequently. § Gradually add the stock and cook for 10–15 minutes. § Transfer the meat to a heated serving dish. § Stir the mustard into the sauce left in the pan. Mix well. § Spoon the mustard sauce over the hamburgers and serve hot with potato purée and a green salad

Scaloppine alla pizzaiola
Veal scaloppine with pizza topping

Serves: 4; Preparation: 25 minutes; Cooking: 15 minutes; Level of difficulty: Simple

Remove any small pieces of fat from the scaloppine. § Pound the meat lightly, dredge in the flour, then shake thoroughly. § Heat the oil in a large sauté pan and brown the scaloppine on both sides. § Season with salt and pepper and sprinkle with the garlic and the capers. Cover each slice with a little tomato sauce and cook for 10–12 minutes (no longer, as the meat will become tough). § Sprinkle with the parsley and serve hot with boiled spinach or Swiss chard briefly sautéed in finely chopped garlic and extra-virgin olive oil.

VARIATION
– During the last 3–4 minutes of cooking, place a thin slice of Mozzarella cheese on top of each scaloppine.

■ INGREDIENTS

- 1¼ lb (600 g) small, thinly sliced veal scaloppine (cut from rump)
- 1 cup (4 oz/125 g) all-purpose (plain) flour
- ⅓ cup (3½ fl oz/100 ml) extra-virgin olive oil
- salt and freshly ground black pepper
- 2 cloves garlic, finely chopped
- 1 tablespoon capers, coarsely chopped
- 2 tablespoons parsley, finely chopped
- 1¼ cups (10 fl oz/300 g) *Simple tomato sauce* (see recipe p. 16)

Wine: a dry red (Sangiovese)

Vitello tonnato
Cold veal with tuna sauce

This wonderful dish requires careful preparation, but the end result is well worth the effort. Firstly, the veal needs to cool in its cooking water (to stop it from becoming tough). Furthermore, the sauce should be spooned over the cool meat and left for several hours before serving. Prepare it a day ahead, so that the veal and tuna sauce are fully blended.

Serves: 4; Preparation: 25 minutes + 6 hours to macerate; Cooking: 2 hours; Level of difficulty: Medium

Remove any fat from the meat and tie firmly with kitchen string. § Put the meat, carrot, celery, bay leaf, and onion stuck with the cloves in a pot with just enough boiling water to cover the meat. Season with salt, cover, and simmer for 2 hours. Leave the veal to cool in its cooking water. § Prepare the mayonnaise. § Drain the oil from the tuna and place the fish in a food processor with the mayonnaise, capers, lemon juice, oil, salt, and pepper. Mix until smooth. § Slice the veal thinly, transfer to a serving dish, and spoon the sauce over the top. Garnish with capers and slices of lemon. Set aside for at least 6 hours. § Serve by itself as an appetizer or with boiled vegetables as a light lunch or main course.

VARIATION
– Add 4 anchovy fillets and 6 pickled gherkins when making the sauce.

■ INGREDIENTS

- 2 lb (1 kg) lean veal roast, preferably rump
- 1 carrot
- 1 stalk celery
- 1 bay leaf
- 1 onion
- 2 cloves
- salt and freshly ground black pepper
- 1 quantity *Mayonnaise* (see recipe p. 18)
- ¾ cup (5 oz/150 g) tuna, packed in oil
- 2 tablespoons capers, plus some to garnish
- juice of 1 lemon, plus ½ lemon to garnish
- 4 tablespoons extra-virgin olive oil

Wine: a dry, sparkling white (Prosecco di Conegliano)

Right: *Scaloppine alla pizzaiola*

INVOLTINI AI CARCIOFI
Beef rolls with artichokes

Serves: 6; Preparation: 25 minutes; Cooking: 20 minutes; Level of difficulty: Medium

Remove any small pieces of fat from the beef and pound lightly. § Beat the eggs in a small bowl with the parsley, garlic, and salt. § Heat 2 tablespoons of oil in a small sauté pan, pour in the egg mixture and cook until firm on both sides. Set aside to cool. § To clean the artichokes, remove the tough outer leaves and trim the tops and stalks. Wash well in cold water and lemon juice. Cut each artichoke into 6 segments. § Heat 2 tablespoons of oil in a sauté pan over medium heat and cook the artichokes for 5 minutes. Season with salt and pepper and set aside. § To prepare the rolls, lay the slices of meat on a work surface and place a piece of mortadella on each. § Cut the cooked egg into 18 pieces. Place a piece of egg and a segment of artichoke on the mortadella. § Roll the meat into filled rolls and close with a toothpick. § Dredge in the flour and place in a sauté pan with the remaining oil. Sprinkle with salt and pepper, and brown on all sides. § Pour in the wine and cook for 20 minutes, adding stock if the pan becomes too dry. § Serve hot with potato purée or braised lentils.

VARIATIONS
– Replace the egg mixture with thin slices of Fontina cheese.
– Use a single, large slice of meat, fill with the same ingredients to make a roll. Cooking time will increase by 30 minutes.

MEDAGLIONE DI FILETTO PROFUMATE ALL'ACETO BALSAMICO
Slices of tenderloin with balsamic vinegar

This quick and simple dish always makes a good impression, even for elegant dinner parties.

Serves: 4; Preparation: 10 minutes; Cooking: 10 minutes; Level of difficulty: Simple

Melt the butter in a heavy-bottomed pan over high heat. When it is foaming, add the shallot and then the meat. Cook for about 4 minutes each side. § Pour in the balsamic vinegar and season with salt and pepper. Cook for 1–2 minutes more. § Set the meat aside in a warm oven. § Return the cooking juices to the heat until they foam, then stir in the cornstarch. § Pour the sauce over the meat and serve hot with a green salad.

■ INGREDIENTS

• 1¼ lb (600 g) beef rump sliced extra thin (18 slices)
• 4 eggs
• 1 tablespoon parsley and garlic, finely chopped
• salt and freshly ground black pepper
• ½ cup (4 fl oz/125 ml) extra-virgin olive oil
• 3 globe artichokes
• juice of ½ lemon
• 5 oz (150 g) mortadella slices, cut in half (18 pieces)
• 3 tablespoons all-purpose (plain) flour
• ½ cup (4 fl oz/125 ml) dry white wine
• ½ cup (4 fl oz/125 ml) *Beef stock* (see recipe p. 22)

Wine: a dry red (Chianti Classico)

■ INGREDIENTS

• 2 tablespoons butter
• ½ shallot, finely chopped
• 4 slices of tenderloin beef, weighing about 5 oz (150 g) each
• ½ cup (4 fl oz/125 ml) balsamic vinegar
• salt and freshly ground black pepper
• 1 tablespoon cornstarch (corn flour)

Wine: a dry, fruity red (Teroldego Rotaliano)

Right: *Involtini ai carciofi*

■ INGREDIENTS

• ⅓ cup (3½ fl oz/100 ml)
  extra-virgin olive oil
• 1 clove garlic, 1 onion,
  1 carrot, 1 stalk celery,
  all finely chopped
• 2 medium tomatoes,
  peeled and chopped
• 1 tablespoon mixed herbs
  (sage, parsley, oregano,
  rosemary, thyme),
  chopped
• 1½ lb (750 g) beef chuck
  with muscle, cut into
  bite-sized pieces
• salt and freshly ground
  black pepper
• ¾ cup (7 fl oz/200 ml)
  red wine
• 2 cups (16 fl oz/500 ml)
  Beef stock (see recipe p. 22)
• 1¼ lb (600 g) potatoes,
  peeled and cut in bite-
  sized chunks

Wine: a dry red (Trentino Rosso)

■ INGREDIENTS

• 10 oz (300 g) asparagus
• 1 shallot, chopped
• 4 tablespoons extra-virgin
  olive oil + 2 tablespoons
• salt and freshly ground
  black pepper
• 3½ tablespoons dry white
  wine
• ¾ cup (6 fl oz/180 ml) Beef
  stock (see recipe p. 22)
• 14 oz (400 g) beef
  carpaccio (see p. 13)

Wine: a dry white
(Vermentino di Argiolas)

Left: Carpaccio tiepido agli asparagi

Spezzatino con patate alla contadina
Farmhouse stew with potatoes

Serves: 6; Preparation: 25 minutes; Cooking: 1 hour and 10 minutes; Level of difficulty: Simple
Heat the oil in a large, heavy-bottomed pan and add the chopped vegetables and herbs. Sauté briefly. § Remove any little pieces of fat from the meat. Add the meat to the pan, season with salt and pepper, and cook until brown. § Pour in the wine and cook until it evaporates. § Cover the pan and simmer for about 1 hour, gradually adding the stock. Stir frequently, to stop the meat from sticking to the pan. § Add the potatoes about 30 minutes before the meat is cooked. § Serve hot.

VARIATION
– Double the quantity of garlic, onion, carrot, and celery, and chop coarsely (instead of finely). Halve the quantity of potatoes or omit them entirely.

Carpaccio tiepido agli asparagi
Carpaccio with asparagus

Serves 4; Preparation: 15 minutes; Cooking: 25 minutes; Level of difficulty: Simple
Wash and dry the asparagus and cut the stems into ½-in (1-cm) thick slices. Leave the tips whole. § Sauté the shallot in 4 tablespoons of oil over medium heat. § When the shallot is transparent, add the asparagus and season with salt and pepper. § Pour in the wine and cook until it evaporates. § Add half the stock and cook for 20 minutes, adding more stock during cooking if the sauce dries out too much. § Remove from heat when the asparagus is cooked but still crunchy. § Arrange the slices of carpaccio on four dinner plates. Season with salt and pepper and drizzle with the remaining oil. § Spoon the hot asparagus and sauce over the meat and serve immediately.

Scaloppine al parmigiano e pomodoro fresco
Veal scaloppine with Parmesan and fresh tomatoes

Serves: 4; Preparation: 25 minutes; Cooking: 25 minutes; Level of difficulty: Simple

Remove any little pieces of fat from the meat. § Cover with foil and pound lightly. § Dredge in the flour, then shake to eliminate any excess. § Heat the oil and butter in a large sauté pan over medium heat. Add the scaloppine and season with salt and pepper. Brown on both sides. § Pour in the wine and cook until it evaporates. § Remove the slices of meat and set aside in a warm oven. § Add the shallots to the pan and lightly brown. § Add the tomatoes, salt, and pepper to taste, and cook until the tomatoes reduce. § Add the scaloppine and sprinkle with the Parmesan, parsley, and basil. § Turn off the heat, cover, and leave to stand for a few minutes. § Serve hot or at room temperature with a green salad.

■ INGREDIENTS

- 8 veal scaloppine, about 12 oz (350 g)
- ½ cup (2 oz/60 g) all-purpose (plain) flour
- 4 tablespoons extra-virgin olive oil
- 2 tablespoons butter
- salt and freshly ground black pepper
- ½ cup (4 fl oz/125 ml) dry white wine
- 2 shallots, coarsely chopped
- 10 oz (300 g) tomatoes, peeled and diced
- 4 oz (125 g) Parmesan cheese, flaked
- 1½ tablespoons each parsley and basil, finely chopped

Wine: a dry white (Pinot Bianco)

Bollito misto alle tre salse
Mixed boiled meats with three sauces

I have suggested three sauces that go particularly well with mixed boiled meats. Try the Onion sauce *(see p. 20),* Hot tomato sauce *(see p. 16) and the* Tartare sauce *(see p. 18) too.*

Serves: 12; Preparation: 25 minutes; Cooking: 1½ hours; Level of difficulty: Simple

Fill a large saucepan with cold water and add the onion, carrot, celery, parsley, half the peppercorns, and a scant teaspoon of salt (use less to be on the safe side; you can always add more, if necessary). § When the water is boiling, add the beef. Simmer for 1½ hours. § After 30 minutes, add the chicken and veal to the saucepan with the beef. § In another saucepan, cover the tongue with cold water and add the wine, bay leaves, and remaining peppercorns. Bring to a boil and then simmer for 1 hour. § When the meats are cooked, break into pieces (except for the

■ INGREDIENTS

- 1 large onion, cut in 4
- 1 carrot, cut in 4
- 1 stalk celery, cut in 2
- 2 sprigs parsley
- 2 teaspoons black peppercorns
- salt
- 2 lb (1 kg) boneless beef brisket or chuck
- 1 chicken, about 2 lb (1 kg)
- 2 lb (1 kg) veal breast with short ribs
- 1 beef tongue, about 2 lb (1 kg)

Right: *Scaloppine al parmigiano e pomodoro fresco*

- ½ cup (4 fl oz/125 ml) dry white wine
- 2 bay leaves
- 1 quantity *Mustard sauce* (see recipe p. 20)
- 1 quantity *Garlic mayonnaise* (see recipe p. 18)
- 1 quantity *Parsley sauce with capers, anchovies, garlic, and oil* (see recipe p. 22)

Wine: a dry red (Chianti Classico)

tongue, which should be sliced) and arrange on a large heated serving dish. Moisten with a ladleful of boiling stock. § While the meat is cooking, prepare (or reheat) the three sauces. Put them in separate serving bowls. § Serve the meats with a platter of mixed boiled vegetables, such as potatoes, carrots, zucchini (courgettes), fennel, and globe artichokes.

VARIATION
— Sieve the beef and chicken stock and use it to make soups, *stracciatella* (stock with egg and cheese), or tortellini in stock. If there is any left over, pour into glass bottles and keep in the refrigerator. It will keep for 3 or 4 days.

Ossibuchi alla milanese
Milanese-style stewed veal shanks

Ossobuco means "bone with a hole" which perfectly describes the calf's hind shank used in this classic Milanese dish. For those who like it, the bone marrow is considered a special delicacy. Gremolada, a mixture of lemon peel, garlic, and parsley, is traditionally added just before removing from the heat. It is optional.

Serves: 4-6; Preparation: 25 minutes; Cooking: 1¾ hours; Level of difficulty: Medium

Make 4–5 incisions around the edge of each shank to stop them curling up during cooking. § Dredge the shanks in the flour and sprinkle with salt and pepper. § Heat the oil in a large, heavy-bottomed saucepan over medium-high heat and cook the shanks briefly on both sides. Remove and set aside. § Melt the butter in the pan and add the carrot, onion, celery, and sage. § When the vegetables are soft, add the meat and cook for a few minutes. § Pour in the wine. When the wine has evaporated, add the stock and tomatoes, and season with salt and pepper to taste. § Cover and simmer over low heat for 1½ hours, adding extra stock if necessary. § When cooked, stir in the lemon peel, garlic, and parsley, if liked. § Transfer to a heated serving dish and serve hot with classic Milanese-style risotto.

INGREDIENTS
- 6 veal hind shanks, cut in 1½-in (4-cm) thick slices
- ½ cup (2 oz/60 g) all-purpose (plain) flour
- salt and freshly ground black pepper
- 4 tablespoons extra-virgin olive oil
- 3 tablespoons butter
- 1 carrot, 1 onion, 1 stalk celery, all finely chopped
- 4 sage leaves, torn
- ¾ cup (7 fl oz/200 ml) dry white wine
- 1 cup (8 fl oz/250 ml) *Beef stock (see recipe p. 22)*
- 3 tablespoons tomatoes, peeled and diced, or *Simple tomato sauce (see recipe p. 16)*
For the *gremolada* (optional)
- peel of 1 lemon, 1 clove garlic, 1 tablespoon parsley, all finely chopped

Wine: a dry red (Chianti Classico Ruffino)

Tartara semplice
Simple tartare

The success of this dish depends on the quality and freshness of the ingredients.

Serves 4; Preparation: 15 minutes; Level of difficulty: Simple

Remove any fat from the meat and chop very finely using a large, sharp knife. Do not buy the meat already ground; it must be freshly chopped. § Mix the olive oil, lemon juice and scallion, if liked, and stir into the meat. § Add the egg yolks and season with salt and pepper. § Divide the meat into 4 portions and shape each one into a sort of meatball. § Serve immediately (otherwise the meat will turn an ugly dark shade of red), with a platter of coarsely raw vegetables (tomatoes, radishes, carrots, fennel, celery, and whatever else you have available in the refrigerator or garden).

INGREDIENTS
- 1 lb/500 g very lean beef (rump)
- 4 tablespoons extra-virgin olive oil
- juice of 2 lemons
- 1 scallion (spring onion), chopped (optional)
- 4 very fresh egg yolks
- salt and freshly ground black pepper

Wine: a dry rosé (Bolgheri Rosato)

Right:
Ossibuchi alla milanese

Magatello glassato con champignons
Glazed topside with mushrooms sautéed in garlic and parsley

Serves: 6; Preparation: 25 minutes; Cooking: 1½ hours; Level of difficulty: Medium

Sprinkle the meat with salt and pepper. Transfer to a roasting pan and drizzle with 5 tablespoons of the oil. Add the whole clove of garlic and the sage and rosemary. § Cook in a preheated oven at 400°F/200°C/gas 6. After about 15 minutes, when the meat is brown all over, pour half the wine over the top and continue cooking for about 1 hour, basting from time to time. If the meat becomes too dry, add more wine or a little stock. § In the meantime, wash the mushrooms under cold running water. Cut off and discard the stems. Peel the mushroom caps and cut into large strips. If the mushrooms are small, leave them whole. § Heat the remaining oil in a sauté pan over medium heat and sauté the chopped garlic and parsley for 2–3 minutes. § Add the mushrooms and sprinkle with salt and pepper. Stir well and cook for 5–7 minutes. § Pour in the remaining wine and cook until it evaporates. Add the stock and cook over medium heat for about 20–25 minutes, or until the liquid reduces, stirring frequently. The mushrooms should be tender, but not mushy. § When the meat is cooked, transfer to a heated serving dish and set aside in a warm place. § Discard the garlic, rosemary, and sage from the cooking juices. Place the sauce over high heat, and stir in the flour. Stir constantly as it thickens, then pour over the meat (the sauce will give it a glazed appearance). § Arrange the mushrooms around the meat and serve hot.

■ INGREDIENTS

- 2½ lb (1.2 kg) slice of veal or beef, preferably rump, rolled and tied with kitchen string
- salt and freshly ground black pepper
- ½ cup (4 fl oz/125 ml) extra-virgin olive oil
- 3 cloves garlic (1 whole, 2 finely chopped)
- 1 twig sage
- 1 twig rosemary
- 1 cup (8 fl oz/250 ml) dry white wine
- 1 cup (8 fl oz/250 ml) *Beef stock (see recipe p. 22)*
- 1½ lb (750 g) white mushrooms
- 1 tablespoon parsley, finely chopped
- 2 tablespoons flour

*Wine: a dry red
(Chianti dei Colli Fiorentini)*

Tasca di vitello farcita alla provola affumicata
Veal roll stuffed with smoked Provola cheese

Serves: 6; Preparation: 20 minutes; Cooking: 1 hour; Level of difficulty: Simple

Make a deep incision in the veal with a sharp knife and open a "pocket" in the meat. § Fill with the cubes of Provola and ham. § Close the meat around the cheese and ham and sew up with a needle and kitchen thread. § Transfer to an ovenproof dish with the oil, rosemary, and garlic. § Sprinkle with salt and pepper, and place in a preheated oven at 400°F/200°C/gas 6. § After 5 minutes, pour the

■ INGREDIENTS

- 1 lb (500 g) piece of veal, preferably rump
- 5 oz (150 g) smoked Provola cheese, cubed
- 5 oz (150 g) ham, cubed
- ½ cup (4 fl oz/125 ml) dry white wine

Right:
Magatello glassato con champignons

- ¾ cup (7 fl oz/200 ml)
  Beef stock (see recipe p. 22)
- ⅓ cup (3½ fl oz/100 ml)
  extra-virgin olive oil
- salt and freshly ground
  black pepper
- 1 sprig rosemary
- 1 clove garlic

*Wine: a dry red
(Merlot)*

wine over the meat and cook for another 55 minutes, basting from time to time. If the meat becomes too dry, add a little stock. § When cooked, discard the kitchen thread and cut the meat into rather thick slices. The Provola should be almost completely melted. § Arrange the slices on a heated serving dish and spoon the sauce over the top. Serve hot with lightly boiled artichokes sautéed briefly in garlic, oil, and parsley.

Stufato di manzo ai funghi porcini
Beef stew with porcini mushrooms

If you can't get fresh porcini, use the same quantity of white mushrooms mixed with 2 tablespoons of dried porcini soaked in warm water for 15–20 minutes.

Serves: 4; Preparation: 25 minutes; Cooking: 1¼ hours; Level of difficulty: Simple

Remove any small pieces of fat from the meat. § Sauté the garlic and onion in the oil in a heavy-bottomed pan (preferably earthenware) over medium heat. § Add the meat when the onion is soft. Season with salt and pepper and simmer in the liquid produced by the meat. § When this liquid has reduced, pour in the wine and cook until it has evaporated. § Add the tomato sauce, stir well and simmer gently over medium-low heat. § In the meantime, clean and wash the mushrooms. Cut the caps into thick strips and the stems into chunks. § Add the mushrooms and mint to the stew after about 40 minutes. Partially cover the pan and simmer until cooked, stirring frequently. Add a little stock if the sauce dries out too much. § Serve hot with potato purée and a mixed salad.

◼ INGREDIENTS

- 1¾ lb (800 g) boneless beef chuck, cut into bite-sized pieces
- 1 clove garlic, finely chopped
- 1 onion, finely chopped
- 4 tablespoons extra-virgin olive oil
- salt and freshly ground black pepper
- ½ cup (4 fl oz/125 ml) dry white wine
- ½ quantity *Simple tomato sauce* (see recipe p. 16)
- 1½ lb (750 g) porcini mushrooms
- 2 sprigs mint
- 1 cup (8 fl oz/250 ml) *Beef stock* (see recipe p. 22)

Wine: a dry red (Barbera d'Asti)

Scaloppine di vitello al limone
Veal scaloppine in lemon sauce

Serves: 4; Preparation: 15 minutes; Cooking: 12–15 minutes; Level of difficulty: Simple

Remove any small pieces of fat from the meat. § Cover with foil (to prevent the veal from breaking), and pound lightly. § Dredge the scaloppine in the flour, shaking off any excess. § Sauté the veal in the butter and oil in a heavy-bottomed pan over high heat, turning often until both sides are evenly browned. Season with salt and pepper. § Lower the heat to medium and continue cooking, adding a little stock to moisten. § After about 12 minutes, when the veal is cooked, turn off the heat and pour the lemon juice over the top. § Sprinkle with the parsley and serve hot with glazed carrots (carrots cooked whole in butter, beef stock, salt, parsley, and a teaspoon of sugar).

VARIATION
– Transfer the cooked scaloppine to a heated serving dish. Add ½ cup (4 fl oz/125 ml) of Marsala wine to the juices left in the pan, and reduce over medium-high heat. Pour the Marsala sauce over the veal and serve immediately.

◼ INGREDIENTS

- 8 veal scaloppine, about 1 lb (500 g)
- ½ cup (2 oz/60 g) all-purpose (plain) flour
- 2½ tablespoons butter
- 2 tablespoons extra virgin olive oil
- salt and freshly ground black pepper
- ½ cup (4 fl oz/125 ml) *Beef stock* (see recipe p. 22)
- juice of 1 lemon
- 1 tablespoon parsley, finely chopped

Wine: a dry white (Orvieto Classico)

Right:
Scaloppine di vitello al limone

■ INGREDIENTS

- 1 lb (500 g) lean ground veal
- 1 egg
- 1 thick slice mortadella, finely chopped
- dash of nutmeg (optional)
- 2 tablespoons bread, soaked in milk and squeezed thoroughly
- 1 clove garlic, finely chopped
- 2 tablespoons parsley, finely chopped
- salt and freshly ground black pepper
- 4 tablespoons all-purpose (plain) flour
- ½ cup (4 fl oz/125 ml) extra-virgin olive oil
- 1 tablespoon butter
- ½ onion, finely chopped
- 1 small carrot, finely chopped
- 1 small stalk celery, finely chopped
- 10 oz (300 g) tomatoes, peeled and chopped, or 1 quantity *Simple tomato sauce* (see recipe p. 16)
- 1 cup (8 fl oz/250 ml) *Beef stock* (see recipe p. 22)

Wine: a dry red (Brusco dei Barbi)

POLPETTONE AL POMODORO
Meat loaf with tomato sauce

Serves: 6; Preparation: 30 minutes; Cooking: 1¼ hours; Level of difficulty: Medium

Mix the veal with the egg, mortadella, nutmeg, bread, garlic, and parsley in a bowl. Season with salt and pepper. § Shape the mixture into a meat loaf. § Put the flour in a large dish and carefully roll the meat loaf in it. § Heat 4 tablespoons of oil in a large, heavy-bottomed pan over medium heat and brown the meat loaf on all sides. Use a fork (but don't prick or pierce the surface) and a wooden spatula when turning. This is the most delicate moment; when the meat loaf is most likely to crumble or break. § The meat will take about 10 minutes to brown. § Drain the meat loaf of the cooking oil and set aside. § In the meantime, heat the butter and the remaining oil in a sauté pan. Add the onion, carrot, celery, and parsley and sauté for 4–5 minutes. § Add the tomatoes (or tomato sauce) and cook for 5 minutes. § Place the meat loaf in the pan and season with salt and pepper. § Partially cover the pan and simmer over low heat for just under 1 hour. Stir frequently, so that the meat loaf does not stick to the bottom. § If the sauce becomes too dense, add a few ladlefuls of stock. § When cooked, set aside to cool. The meat loaf should only be sliced when almost cold, otherwise the slices may break. § Arrange the sliced meat loaf on a serving dish. Heat the sauce just before serving and pour over the slices. Serve with potato purée or mixed stir-fried vegetables.

VARIATIONS
– Omit the tomatoes or tomato sauce and serve the meat loaf with the juice of half a lemon.
– For a Piemontese-style meat loaf, omit the tomatoes or tomato sauce. Place two shelled hard-cooked (hard-boiled) eggs inside the loaf when shaping it. It will be much more attractive when sliced.

Left: Polpettone al pomodoro

Polpettine Elda
Elda's meatballs

This recipe was given to me by my mother-in-law, Elda.
Simple and hearty, these meatballs make a wonderful family meal.

Serves: 4; Preparation: 20 minutes; Cooking: 25 minutes; Level of difficulty: Simple

Combine the meat, egg, bread soaked in milk, salt, and pepper in a bowl. Mix well until the mixture is firm. § Take egg-sized pieces of the mixture and shape them into oval meatballs. Coat them in bread crumbs and then flatten slightly. § Heat the oil in a large, heavy-bottomed pan over medium heat. § Add the meatballs when the oil is very hot (but not smoking) and fry until brown on both sides. § Moisten with the stock and cook until it evaporates. § Taste for salt and pepper. § Add the milk and cook until it reduces, forming a dense cream. § Serve hot with boiled peas, dotted with butter and sprinkled with parsley.

VARIATION
– The meatballs can be prepared ahead of time. When they are coated in bread crumbs, transfer to a plate, cover with plastic wrap and place in the refrigerator. They will keep for 1–2 days.

■ INGREDIENTS

- 12 oz (350 g) lean ground veal
- 1 egg
- 1 heaped tablespoon bread, soaked in milk and thoroughly squeezed
- salt and freshly ground black pepper
- 1 cup (4 oz/125 g) bread crumbs
- 4 tablespoons extra-virgin olive oil
- ½ cup (4 fl oz/125 ml) *Beef stock (see recipe p. 22)*
- ½ cup (4 fl oz/125 ml) milk

Wine: a dry white
(Bianco di Franciacorta)

Scannello ai capperi e acciughe
Sirloin with capers and anchovies

Serves: 6; Preparation: 20 minutes; Cooking: 35-40 minutes; Level of difficulty: Medium

Place the meat in a large, heavy-bottomed pan with the oil over high heat. Brown on both sides. § Add the onion, carrot, and celery, and sprinkle with a little salt and pepper (be sure not to add too much salt — the anchovies to be added later can be quite salty). Stir well and cook for 4–5 minutes. § Pour in the wine, partially cover, and cook for about 30 minutes, turning the meat often. § When the meat is tender, set aside on a chopping board, ready to be sliced. § Turn off the heat and add the capers and anchovies to the vegetables. Mix well and purée in a food

■ INGREDIENTS

- 2½ lb (1.2 kg) sirloin
- ⅓ cup (3½ fl oz/100 ml) extra-virgin olive oil
- 1 onion, coarsely chopped
- 1 carrot, coarsely chopped
- 1 stick celery, coarsely chopped
- salt and freshly ground black pepper
- 1 heaped tablespoon capers

Right:
Scannello ai capperi e acciughe

- 2 anchovy fillets, well cleaned and washed
- ½ cup (4 fl oz/125 ml) dry white wine
- ½ cup (4 fl oz/125 ml) *Beef stock* (see recipe p. 22)

Wine: a dry red (Aprilia Merlot)

processor or food mill, to make a thick vegetable cream. § Slice the sirloin and arrange on a heated serving dish. Spoon the sauce over the top and serve hot. Serve with potato purée.

VARIATION
— For a simpler dish, or if you don't like capers and anchovies, omit them. In this case, season the mashed vegetables with a little freshly ground nutmeg.

INGREDIENTS

- 2 large potatoes, boiled
- 13 oz (400 g) boiled brisket or chuck
- 2 eggs
- 1 tablespoon parsley, finely chopped
- 1 clove garlic, finely chopped
- salt and freshly ground black pepper
- 1 cup (4 oz/125 g) bread crumbs
- ½ cup (4 fl oz/125 ml) oil for frying

Wine: a dry rosé
(Rosé Antinori)

POLPETTINE DI LESSO E PATATE
Boiled meat and potato meatballs

Serves: 4; Preparation: 25 minutes; Cooking: 20-25 minutes; Level of difficulty: Medium

Mash the potatoes in a food mill or with a potato masher. Do not use a food processor because the mixture will become too sticky and the meatballs will be difficult to fry. Transfer the mixture to a bowl. § In the meantime, grind the boiled meat in a food processor. § Add to the bowl with the potatoes. § Stir in one egg, the parsley, and garlic. Season with salt and pepper, and mix well. The mixture should be quite dense, but if it is too dry, add the other egg. § Shape the mixture into oblong meatballs (like croquettes), and roll them in bread crumbs. § Heat the oil in a heavy-bottomed pan until hot (but not smoking) and fry the meatballs until they are golden brown. § Drain on paper towels. Sprinkle with salt and serve hot with a fresh, green salad.

INGREDIENTS

- 8 veal loin chops, about 1 lb (500 g)
- 2 eggs
- salt
- ⅓ cup (1¼ oz/40 g) all-purpose (plain) flour
- 1 cup (4 oz/125 g) bread crumbs
- ½ cup (4 fl oz/125 ml) oil for frying
- ½ cup (4 oz/125 g) butter
- 1 tablespoon anchovy paste

Wine: red
(Trentino Marzemino)

COSTOLETTE FRITTE ALLA MILANESE CON ACCIUGATA
Fried Milanese-style chops with anchovy sauce

Serves: 4; Preparation: 20 minutes; Cooking: 10 minutes; Level of difficulty: Simple

Rinse the chops under cold running water and pat dry with paper towels. Make little cuts around the edges to stop them from curling up during cooking. §. Lightly coat the chops with flour, shaking off any excess. § Beat the eggs in a bowl with the salt. Dip the chops in the beaten egg, then coat with bread crumbs, making sure that they stick to the chops. § Heat the oil in a heavy-bottomed pan until very hot and fry the chops. Fry over medium heat, so that the meat is well-cooked right through and not burnt on the outside. The bread crumbs should be golden brown and crispy. § Drain the chops on paper towels. § Prepare the anchovy sauce by melting the butter in a small, heavy-bottomed saucepan over low heat. Stir in the anchovy paste. When smooth, spoon over the chops. § Serve hot, with French fries and a green or mixed salad.

Left: Polpettine di lesso e patate

Filetti al pepe verde
Beef fillets with green pepper

Serves: 4; Preparation: 10 minutes; Cooking: 10 minutes; Level of difficulty: Simple

Mash the green peppercorns with a fork. Use your hands to press the crushed peppercorns so that they stick to both sides of the fillets. § Heat the butter and oil in a heavy-bottomed pan. § Season the fillets with salt and add to the pan. § Pour in the cognac and cook until it evaporates. §  Add the cream and cook for about 5 minutes more, turning the meat over at least once. If the sauce is too liquid, remove the fillets and set them aside in a warm oven. Turn up the heat and cook the sauce until it reduces sufficiently. § Arrange the fillets on a heated serving dish and spoon the sauce over the top. § Serve hot with green beans cooked in butter or fennel *au gratin*.

■ INGREDIENTS

- 2 tablespoons soft green peppercorns (in liquid)
- 4 beef fillets, cut 1-in (2.5-cm) thick slices
- 2 tablespoons butter
- 4 tablespoons extra-virgin olive oil
- salt
- ½ cup (4 fl oz/125 ml) cognac (or brandy)
- 2 tablespoons fresh cream

Wine: a dry white (Vernaccia di San Gimignano)

Roast-beef alla senape
Roast beef in mustard sauce

Serves 6; Preparation: 5 minutes; Cooking: 25 minutes; Level of difficulty: Simple

Heat the olive oil in a deep-sided skillet. Sprinkle the beef with a generous coating of pepper and add to the pan. Keeping the heat quite high, allow the meat to brown on both sides. § After 10 minutes turn the heat down and smother the beef with the mustard and brandy, and leave to cook for 15 minutes more. § Be sure to add the salt after the meat is cooked; if it is added before the beef will be less tender. § Thinly slice and serve. Asparagus makes goes well with this dish. For best results, boil the asparagus for 10 minutes, then transfer to an oven-proof dish, add slices of brie, cover and gently heat in the oven.

■ INGREDIENTS

- ½ cup (4 fl oz/125 ml) extra-virgin olive oil
- joint of beef, about 2½ lb (1.2 kg)
- salt and freshly ground black pepper
- 7 oz (200 g) mustard
- 4 tablespoons brandy

Wine: a dry red (Pinot Nero Colli Piacentini)

VARIATIONS
—For this recipe a joint of beef will give the best results, as it does not take long to cook and is always nice and tender.
—Leaving out the mustard and the brandy will give you the classic English roast beef.

Right: *Filetti al pepe verde*

■ INGREDIENTS

- 2 lb (1 kg) lean suckling veal, in bite-sized pieces
- 4 tablespoons extra-virgin olive oil
- 2 cloves garlic, finely chopped
- 2 tablespoons parsley, finely chopped
- ¾ cup (7 fl oz/200 ml) milk
- ½ cup (4 fl oz/125 ml) Beef stock (see recipe p. 22)
- salt and freshly ground black pepper

Wine: a dry white
(Tocai Friulano)

Spezzatino in bianco al prezzemolo
Veal stew with parsley

Serves: 6; Preparation: 15 minutes; Cooking: about 1 hour; Level of difficulty: Simple

Remove any pieces of fat from the veal. § Heat the oil in a large, heavy-bottomed pan over medium heat and sauté the garlic and parsley for 2–3 minutes. § Add the meat and cook in its juices until it reduces. Season with salt and pepper. § Pour in the milk and stock. The meat should be almost, but not completely, covered. Reduce the heat and partially cover the pan, so that the liquid evaporates. Cook very slowly, stirring frequently since the milk tends to stick, until the liquid reduces, forming a dense sauce. § Transfer to a heated serving dish and serve hot with a side dish of lightly boiled peas briefly sautéed in olive oil, garlic, and parsley.

VARIATION
– This stew can be prepared in advance (even the day before), and reheated just before serving.

■ INGREDIENTS

- 1¼ lb (600 g) calf's liver, sliced
- 2 heaped tablespoons all-purpose (plain) flour
- 2 tablespoons extra-virgin olive oil
- 2 cloves garlic, finely chopped
- 10 leaves fresh sage
- salt and freshly ground black pepper

Wine: a dry red
(Chianti dei Colli Fiorentini)

Fegato alla salvia
Sautéed calf's liver with fresh sage

This simple, elegant dish is also known as Fegato alla fiorentina *(Sautéed calf's liver, Florentine-style). It originally comes from the Tuscan capital, although it is becoming more and more difficult to find in the city's trattorias and restaurants.*

Serves: 4; Preparation: 5 minutes; Cooking: 7-10 minutes; Level of difficulty: Simple

Ask your butcher to slice the liver ready for cooking. § Lightly flour the liver and set aside on a plate. § Heat the oil in a large, heavy-bottomed pan and add the garlic and sage. Sauté over medium-high heat for 2 minutes, then add the liver. § Cook until well-browned on both sides. § Serve hot with potato purée and a green salad.

Left:
Spezzatino in bianco al prezzemolo

VARIATION
– Replace the oil with the same amount of butter.

Peposo
Black pepper stew

Serves: 8; Preparation: 10 minutes; Cooking: 3 hours; Level of difficulty: Simple
Place the meat in a large, heavy-bottomed saucepan (preferably earthenware) with the garlic, tomatoes, salt, and pepper. Pour in just enough of the water to cover the meat. § Cook over medium heat for 2 hours, adding extra water if the sauce becomes too dry. Stir from time to time. § After 2 hours, pour in the wine and cook for 1 hour more, or until the meat is very tender. § Serve hot with mixed boiled vegetables.

Piccoli spiedini misti di carne e verdure
Mixed meat and vegetable skewers

There are many variations on the traditional recipe for mixed meat and vegetable skewers. The basic dish calls for bite-sized chunks of two or three different meats alternated with cherry tomatoes, baby onions, bell peppers, and bread. Always place the bread next to the meat, so that it absorbs the cooking juices. The crisp, mouthwatering pieces of roasted bread are one of the best parts of this dish. These skewers are also very good when cooked over a barbecue.

Serves: 6; Preparation: 1 hour; Cooking: 30 minutes; Level of difficulty: Medium
Remove any fat from the meat. § Chop the meat, vegetables, and bread into large cubes or squares. Slice the sausages thickly. § Thread the cubes onto wooden skewers, alternating pieces of meat, sausage, vegetables, bread, and sage leaves. § Arrange the skewers in a roasting dish and season with salt and pepper. Drizzle with the oil. § Bake in a preheated oven at 400°F/200°C/gas 6 for 30 minutes, turning occasionally and adding beef stock to moisten, if required. § When the meat is well browned, remove from the oven and serve hot. These skewers are particularly good when served with a dish of hot polenta.

■ INGREDIENTS

- 3½ lb (1.7 kg) muscle from veal shanks, cut in bite-sized pieces
- 4 cloves garlic, finely chopped
- 1¼ lb (600 g) tomatoes, peeled and chopped
- salt
- 3 tablespoons freshly ground black pepper
- 4 cups (2 pints/1 liter) cold water
- 1½ cups (12 fl oz/350 ml) robust, dry red wine

Wine: a dry red (Carmignano)

■ INGREDIENTS

- 3 fresh Italian pork sausages
- 10 oz (300 g) of pork
- 12 oz (350 g) boned veal, shoulder, or shank
- 1 lb (500 g) chicken breast
- 1 yellow and 1 red bell pepper (capsicum)
- 10 oz (300 g) baby onions
- 20 cherry tomatoes
- 5 slices crusty bread
- 10 leaves fresh sage
- salt and freshly ground black pepper
- ¼ cup (2 fl oz/60 ml) extra-virgin olive oil

Wine: a dry red (Santa Cristina)

Right:
Peposo

Pork

Succulent pork is always good as a simple roast, but it also combines well with a wide range of vegetables and fruit.

Filetto di maiale alle mele
Fillet of pork with apple

Pork is always good in sweet-and-sour dishes with fruit like apples or prunes.
This dish, hearty and easy-to-prepare, is perfect for cold winter evenings.

Serves: 4; Preparation: 5 minutes + 2 hours marinating; Cooking: 1 hour; Level of difficulty: Simple

Cut the apples in half and remove the cores. Place in a bowl, cover with the wine, and set aside to marinate for at least 2 hours (you may leave them even longer if you have the time). § Season the pork with salt and pepper and transfer to a baking pan with the oil. § Bake in a preheated oven at 400°F/200°C/gas 6. After 10 minutes, pour about half the wine used to marinate the apples over the pork. Turn the pork and cook for another 20 minutes. § Arrange the apples around the pork in the baking pan and add more wine if the pan is dry. Cook for 30 minutes more. § Slice the pork and transfer to a serving dish. Arrange the apples around the pork and serve hot with a bowl of steaming potato purée.

■ INGREDIENTS

• 6 Golden Delicious apples
• 2 cups (16 fl oz/500 ml) dry white wine
• 2 pork fillets, about 1 lb (500 g)
• salt and freshly ground black pepper
• 4 tablespoons extra-virgin olive oil

Wine: a dry red (Freisa)

Arista arrosto
Pan-roasted pork with potatoes

In Tuscany pork loin with ribs is known as "arista." This dish is normally eaten cold and can be cooked the day before.

Serves: 6; Preparation: 20 minutes; Cooking: 1½ hours; Level of difficulty: Simple

Detach the loin from the ribs. Use a sharp knife to make fairly deep incisions in the loin and fill with the garlic, rosemary, and sage mixed with salt and pepper. § Tie the ribs to the loin with 2 or 3 twists of kitchen string. The ribs will make the dish tastier. § Heat the butter and oil in a heavy-bottomed pan over medium heat. § Add the meat and brown all over. § Pour a ladle of stock over the top, cover, and continue cooking, adding the stock gradually to keep the pan moist. § Peel the potatoes and cut them into bite-sized pieces. § When the pork has been cooking for 30 minutes, add the potatoes and unpeeled cloves of garlic. § When cooked, untie the ribs and arrange the meat and potatoes in a heated serving dish. The cooking juices can be spooned over the top or served separately.

■ INGREDIENTS

• 2 lb (1 kg) pork loin rib roast
• 2 cloves garlic, finely chopped
• 1 tablespoon rosemary, finely chopped
• 1 tablespoon sage, finely chopped
• salt and freshly ground black pepper
• 1 tablespoon butter
• ½ cup (4 fl oz/125 ml) extra-virgin olive oil
• 4 cups (2 pints/1 liter) *Beef stock (see recipe p. 22)*
• 2 lb (1 kg) potatoes
• 2 cloves garlic, unpeeled

Right: Filetto di maiale alle mele

■ INGREDIENTS

- 4 tablespoons extra-virgin olive oil
- 2 cloves garlic, chopped
- 4 leaves sage
- 1 lb (500 g) white kidney beans, precooked
- 1 lb (500 g) tomatoes, peeled and diced
- 8 Italian pork sausages
- salt and freshly ground black pepper

Wine: a dry red (Chianti Classico)

Salsicce e fagioli all'uccelletto
Pork sausages and beans with garlic, sage, and tomato sauce

This traditional Tuscan dish is a meal in itself. For best results, use fresh or dried beans (the latter should be soaked for 12 hours) cooked in salted water until tender. Otherwise use high quality canned beans.

Serves: 4; Preparation: 5 minutes; Cooking: 30 minutes; Level of difficulty: Simple

Heat the oil in a heavy-bottomed pan, preferably earthenware, and sauté the garlic and sage. § Add the beans and cook for a few minutes so that they absorb the seasoning. § Add the tomatoes and season with salt and pepper. § Prick the sausages with a fork and add to the beans. Cover and cook over medium-low heat for about 25 minutes, stirring frequently. § Serve hot.

Zampone con lenticchie stufate
Stewed large sausage with lentils

Zampone and cotechino are regional dishes from the city of Modena in Emilia-Romagna. They are large sausages made with a mixture of pork, salt, pepper, nutmeg, cloves, and other seasonings wrapped in pig's trotter for zampone *and in rind from pig snout and jowl for* cotechino. *The large sausage must be soaked in cold water for at least 4 hours before cooking to soften the rind. In Italy this dish is traditionally served on New Year's day.*

Serves: 6; Preparation: 15 minutes + at least 4 hours soaking; Cooking: 3 hours; Level of difficulty: Simple

Soak the sausage in abundant cold water for at least 4 hours. § Drain the sausage and transfer to a pot with enough lightly salted cold water to cover it completely. Cover and simmer gently for 3 hours. Be careful not to puncture the skin during cooking. § In the meantime, prepare the lentils. Sauté the carrot, celery, and onion with the oil in a sauté pan over medium-high heat. § When the vegetables are soft, add the lentils and sauté for 2–3 minutes more. Season with salt and pepper and add the tomatoes. § Cook for a few minutes more, then pour in the stock. Cover and cook for 40 minutes. § Spoon the lentils onto a heated serving dish. Slice the sausage thickly and arrange the slices on the lentils. § Serve hot with a side dish of mashed potatoes.

VARIATION	

VARIATION
– Some excellent precooked *zamponi* and *cotechini* are now available. These do not need to be soaked and they only take about 20–30 minutes to cook.

■ INGREDIENTS

- 1 *zampone* (large sausage wrapped in pig's trotter), about 2 lb (1 kg), or 1¼ lb (600 g) *cotechino* (pork sausage) about 3 in (7.5 cm) in diameter and 8 in (20 cm) long
- salt and freshly ground black pepper
- 5 cups (1 lb/500 g) lentils, precooked
- 1 carrot, finely chopped
- 1 stalk celery, finely chopped
- 1 small onion, finely chopped
- 4 tablespoons extra-virgin olive oil
- 8 oz (250 g) tomatoes, canned
- 2 cups (16 fl oz/500 ml) *Beef stock (see recipe p. 22)*

Wine: a dry red (Gutturnio)

Prosciutto di maiale al Calvados
Ham with Calvados

Serves: 6; Preparation: 2 minutes for the ham + 15 minutes for the mash; Cooking: 1¼ hours; Level of difficulty: Medium

Clean the ham of any small pieces of fat or skin. Season with salt and pepper and bake with the oil in a preheated oven at 400°F/200°C/gas 6. § After 15 minutes, dilute the honey in the orange juice and brush the meat with this mixture. Return to the oven, this time at 375°F/190°C/gas 5. § After 15 minutes turn the ham over, brush with the honey mixture again, and return to the oven. § Repeat this process twice more, before you

■ INGREDIENTS

- 1 ham, 2¼ lb (1.2 kg)
- salt and freshly ground black pepper
- ⅓ cup (3½ fl oz/100 ml) extra-virgin olive oil
- 3 tablespoons honey
- juice of 1 orange

Right:
Zampone con lenticchie stufate

- 6 apples, peeled and in segments
- ½ cup (4 fl oz/125 ml) Calvados liqueur (made with distilled apples)
- 2 lb (1 kg) potatoes
- 2 tablespoons butter

Wine: a dry red (Chianti Classico)

finish cooking. This will take about 1 hour. § In the meantime, halfway through cooking, add the apples to the ham and pour half the Calvados over them. § Wash the potatoes and boil them in their skins in a large pan of salted water. § When the ham is cooked, transfer to a heavy-bottomed pan with its juice and the apples. Place over high heat, pour in the remaining Calvados, and cook until the liqueur has evaporated. § When the potatoes are cooked, drain, peel, and mash. § Mash the apples cooked with the ham, season with salt and butter, and combine with the potatoes. If the mixture is too liquid, add a little flour. Place over low heat, stirring frequently, until thick. § Slice the ham and transfer to a heated serving dish. § Serve hot with the potato and apple purée.

Carré di maiale farcito alle prugne
Pork loin with prunes

Serves: 6; Preparation: 20 minutes + 30 minutes to marinate the prunes; Cooking: 1¼ hours; Level of difficulty: Simple

Place 10 prunes in a bowl with the cognac, diluted with enough water to cover the fruit. Set aside to marinate. § After 30 minutes drain well so that all the marinade has been removed. § Use a sharp knife to make incisions in the pork. Fill with a little salt and pepper and the prunes. § Place the rosemary on the meat and tie with kitchen string. Sprinkle with salt and pepper to taste. § Heat the butter and oil in an ovenproof pan over medium heat. As soon as the butter foams, add the pork and brown all over. § Transfer to a preheated oven at 350°F/180°C/gas 4. § Halfway through cooking, pour the wine over the meat and add the remaining prunes. Continue cooking, adding stock if the pan dries out. § Serve hot or at room temperature with the sauce (heated, if the meat is lukewarm), and prunes. § This dish is delicious served with a side dish of potatoes lightly fried with a finely chopped onion. When the onion and potatoes are golden brown, cover with stock and cook until the stock reduces.

■ INGREDIENTS

- 20–25 dried prunes, pitted
- ½ cup (4 fl oz/125 ml) cognac
- 2 lb (1 kg) boneless pork loin
- salt and freshly ground black pepper
- 4 sprigs rosemary
- 2 tablespoons butter
- 4 tablespoon extra-virgin olive oil
- ¾ cup (7 fl oz/200 ml) dry white wine
- 1 cup (8 fl oz/250 ml) *Beef stock* (see recipe p. 22)

*Wine: a dry red
(Cabernet di Breganze)*

Lonza di maiale al ginepro
Pork loin with juniper berries

Serves: 6; Preparation: 25 minutes + 2 hours to marinate; Cooking: 1½ hours; Level of difficulty: Medium

Marinate the loin for 2 hours, covered with the coarsely sliced shallot, the onion, juniper berries, bay leaves, salt, pepper, 3 tablespoons of oil, and the wine. § After marinating, drain the meat thoroughly and wrap in the pancetta. Tie with a few twists of kitchen string. Transfer to an ovenproof dish. § Strain the vegetables and herbs used in the marinade and add to the meat. § Add the remaining oil and place in a preheated oven at 375°F/190°C/gas 5. § Cook for 1½ hours, basting from time to time with wine from the marinade and turning the meat over every so often. § Slice and serve hot. Strain the cooking juices and spoon over the meat. Serve with baked fennel (lightly boiled fennel baked with béchamel and Parmesan).

■ INGREDIENTS

- 2½ lb (1.2 kg) pork loin (part of loin without bone and without fillet)
- 1 shallot
- 1 onion, chopped
- 10–15 juniper berries
- 2 bay leaves
- salt and freshly ground black pepper
- ⅓ cup (3½ fl oz/100 ml) extra-virgin olive oil
- ½ cup (4 fl oz/125 ml) dry white wine
- 4 oz (125 g) pancetta, sliced

Wine: a dry red (Chianti)

Right: *Carré di maiale farcito alle prugne*

Arista all'aceto e latte
Pork loin with milk and vinegar

Serves: 6; Preparation: 10 minutes; Cooking: 1¼ hours; Level of difficulty: Simple

Season the pork with salt and pepper, and roll and tie with a few twists of kitchen string. § Heat the butter and oil in a heavy-bottomed pan with the rosemary. When the butter foams, add the onion and cook until soft. § Add the pork and lightly brown all over. § Pour the vinegar over the pork and cook until it has evaporated. § Add the milk and the crumbled meat stock cube. Partially cover and cook for 1 hour, turning the meat from time to time. When cooked, the sauce in the pan should be well-reduced and thick. § Slice the pork, transfer to a heated serving dish and spoon the sauce over the top. § Serve hot with boiled new potatoes and green beans.

■ INGREDIENTS

- 2¼ lb (1.2 kg) pork loin, boneless
- salt and freshly ground black pepper
- 2 tablespoons butter
- 4 tablespoons extra-virgin olive oil
- 1 sprig rosemary
- 1 onion, finely chopped
- ¾ cup (7 fl oz/200 ml) white vinegar
- 1¾ cups (14 fl oz/ 450 ml) milk
- 1 beef stock cube

Wine: a young, dry red (Sangiovese di Romagna)

Misto di maiale stufato al vino rosso
Mixed pork stewed in red wine

To make this dish even tastier, replace the canned tomatoes with the same quantity of Simple tomato sauce *(see recipe on p. 16).*

Serves: 6; Preparation: 25 minutes; Cooking: 1½ hours; Level of difficulty: Medium

Ask your butcher to chop each sparerib into 3 pieces. Cut the neck, shanks, and sausages into bite-sized pieces. § Heat the oil in a heavy-bottomed saucepan over medium-high heat. Add the onion, carrot, celery, parsley, and bay leaves and sauté for 3–4 minutes. § Add the pork, season with salt and pepper, and brown all over. § Pour in the wine and cook until it is partially evaporated. § Stir in the tomatoes. § Cover and simmer gently over low heat for about 1¼ hours. Add the stock gradually as the sauce dries out. Turn the meat from time to time. § Serve hot. This dish is traditionally served with polenta.

■ INGREDIENTS

- 3 lb (1.5 kg) mixed cuts of pork (spareribs, boned neck, boneless shanks)
- 3 Italian pork sausages
- ⅓ cup (3½ fl oz/100 ml) extra-virgin olive oil
- 1 onion, 1 carrot, 1 stalk celery, coarsely chopped
- 1 clove garlic, finely chopped
- 1 tablespoon parsley, finely chopped
- 2 bay leaves
- salt and freshly ground black pepper
- ¾ cup (7 fl oz/200 ml) robust red wine
- 12 oz (350 g) canned tomatoes
- 1 cup (8 fl oz/250 ml) *Beef stock (see recipe p. 22)*

Wine: a dry red (Barolo)

Right: *Misto di maiale stufato al vino rosso*

LATTONZOLO AL FORNO
Roast suckling pig with mixed vegetables

Serves: 6; Preparation: 10 minutes; Cooking: 1¾ hours; Level of difficulty: Medium

Sauté the vegetables in a large, heavy-bottomed pan with 2 tablespoons of oil over high heat for 5–6 minutes. § Sprinkle with salt and stir thoroughly. Remove from heat and set aside. § Add the remaining oil to the same pan used for the vegetables and brown the pork. § Transfer the meat and any liquid it has produced to a roasting pan. Sprinkle with a little more salt and the peppercorns. Add the bay leaves and turn the meat in its juices. § Cook in a preheated oven at 400°F/200°C/gas 6 for 1½ hours, basting frequently and gradually adding the wine. § When the pork has been in the oven for about 1 hour, add the vegetables and sprinkle with the garlic and parsley. § When the meat is cooked, it will have a dark, crisp layer of crackling. § Arrange on a heated serving dish with the vegetables and serve hot.

■ INGREDIENTS

• 2 onions, 2 carrots, 2 stalks celery, 2 zucchini (courgettes), 3 potatoes, diced
• 1 leek, sliced
• ⅓ cup (3½ fl oz/100 ml) extra-virgin olive oil
• salt
• ½ suckling pig, about 4 lb (2 kg)
• 10 peppercorns
• 2 bay leaves
• ¾ cup (7 fl oz/200 ml) dry white wine
• 1 tablespoon garlic and parsley, finely chopped

Wine: a dry red (Grignolino)

BISTECCHINE DI MAIALE AL CAVOLO NERO
Pork cutlets with black cabbage

Black cabbage is a special Tuscan vegetable with a strong, slightly bitter taste. It is difficult to find outside Tuscany. However, this dish is just as good when prepared with the same amount of Swiss chard (silver beet). The Swiss chard does not need to be boiled for 30 minutes before chopping; 8–10 minutes will be enough.

Serves: 4; Preparation: 15 minutes; Cooking: 1 hour; Level of difficulty: Simple

Wash the black cabbage, remove the tough stalks, and cook in a pot of salted, boiling water for about 30 minutes. § Drain, and when lukewarm, chop finely. § Sauté the onion and garlic in the oil in a large, heavy-bottomed pan until soft. § Add the cutlets, sprinkle with salt and pepper, and brown on both sides. § Pour in the wine and cook for 15–20 minutes, or until the cutlets are tender. § When the meat is cooked set it aside and add the black cabbage to the cooking juices in the pan. Cook over medium for 10 minutes, stirring frequently. § Return the cutlets to the pan and reheat. § Serve hot.

■ INGREDIENTS

• 1¾ lb (800 g) leaf cabbage
• salt and freshly ground black pepper
• 1 onion, finely chopped
• 1 clove garlic, finely chopped
• 4 tablespoons extra-virgin olive oil
• 4 pork cutlets, about 1¼ lb (600 g)
• ¾ cup (7 fl oz/200 ml) red wine

Wine: a dry red (Velletri Rosso)

Right: Bistecchine di maiale al cavolo nero

■ INGREDIENTS

- 3 pork shanks, weighing about 3 lb (1.5 kg)
- 4 tablespoons flour
- ⅓ cup (3½ fl oz/100 ml) extra-virgin olive oil
- salt and freshly ground black pepper
- ¾ cup (200 ml/7 fl oz) dry white wine
- 2½ cups (13 oz/400 g) carrots, 2 cups (10 oz/300 g) celery, 2 cups (10 oz/300 g) onions, 2½ cups (13 oz/400 g) potatoes, 2 cups (10 oz/300 g) zucchini (courgettes), all peeled and chopped in large dice
- 2 cups (16 fl oz/500 ml) Beef stock (see recipe p. 22)

Wine: a dry red
(Nobile di Montepulciano)

Stinchetti di maiale al forno con verdure miste
Roast pork shanks with mixed vegetables

Serves: 6; Preparation: 50 minutes; Cooking: 2 hours; Level of difficulty: Medium

Remove any remaining hairs from the shanks. Rinse under cold running water and pat dry with paper towels. § Roll in the flour and sprinkle with salt and pepper. § Heat 4 tablespoons of the oil in a large, heavy-bottomed pan, add the shanks and cook over high heat until they are golden brown. § Transfer the shanks and their cooking juices to a roasting pan. Place in a preheated oven at 400°F/200°C/gas 6. § Cook for 20 minutes. Add the wine and cook for 40 minutes more, adding a little stock if the pan becomes too dry. § Meanwhile, heat the remaining oil in a heavy-bottomed pan and sauté the vegetables over high heat for 5–7 minutes. § When the shanks have been in the oven for about 1 hour, add the vegetables and their cooking juices. § Return to the oven and cook for 1 hour more, basting with stock as required to stop the pan from drying out. § When cooked, arrange the meat and vegetables on a heated serving dish and serve hot.

Left: *Stinchetti di maiale al forno con verdure miste*

VARIATION
— If you have the time, lower the oven temperature to 300°F/150°C/gas 2 and extend the second cooking to two hours. Turn the heat up again to 400°F/200°C/gas 6 for 10 minutes just before serving. The pork and vegetables will be even more tender and delicious.

LAMB

Lamb is eaten throughout Italy, but it is more typical of the south and the islands of Sicily and Sardinia.

AGNELLO CON DADOLATA DI MELANZANE
Lamb stew with eggplant

Serves: 4; Preparation: 20 minutes + 2 hours for the eggplants; Cooking: 1¼ hours; Level of difficulty: Medium

Rinse the eggplants under cold running water and, without peeling them, cut into bite-sized cubes. Place in a colander, sprinkle with coarse sea salt, and leave to degorge for about 2 hours. § Heat the oil in a heavy-bottomed pan and sauté the lamb over medium-high heat until golden brown. Season with salt and pepper. § Add the onion and cook for 10 minutes, stirring continually so that it doesn't stick. § Add the eggplant, marjoram, and thyme and cook for 5 minutes. § Pour in the tomato sauce and mix well. § Cover the pan partially and cook over medium-low heat for about 1 hour, adding the stock gradually as the sauce dries out. § Serve hot with new boiled potatoes and a green salad.

■ INGREDIENTS

- 2 eggplants (aubergines)
- 2 tablespoons coarse salt
- 4 tablespoons extra-virgin olive oil
- 2 lb (1 kg) lamb shoulder, cut in 2-in (5-cm) pieces with bone
- salt and freshly ground black pepper
- 1 onion, coarsely chopped
- 1 teaspoon marjoram, 1 teaspoon thyme, finely chopped
- 1 quantity *Simple tomato sauce* (see recipe p. 16)
- 1¼ cups (10 fl oz/300 ml) *Beef stock* (see recipe p. 22)

Wine: a dry red (Barbaresco)

ABBACCHIO ALLA ROMANA
Roman-style, pan-roasted lamb

Pan-roasted, very young lamb is one of the Eternal City's classic dishes. In Rome, the lamb used is never more than a month old. Ideally, it should not have fed on anything stronger than its mother's milk. You will probably not be able to obtain such young lamb; but you can still count on excellent results with slightly older spring lamb.

Serves: 4; Preparation: 25 minutes; Cooking: 1 hour; Level of difficulty: Simple

Cut the lamb into 2-in (5-cm) pieces. § Heat the oil in a heavy-bottomed pan large enough to contain the meat. Add the 2 whole cloves of garlic and the lamb and sauté over medium-high heat until the lamb is golden all over. § Sprinkle with 1 tablespoon of the rosemary and sage and season with salt and pepper. § After about 10 minutes pour in the wine. When it has evaporated, lower the heat, partially cover the pan and continue cooking for about 40 minutes, turning from time to time. § In the meantime, place the anchovies and finely chopped garlic in a bowl with the remaining rosemary and sage and the vinegar. § When the lamb is cooked, raise the heat, pour the vinegar mixture over the top and cook for another 5 minutes. § Serve hot with roast potatoes.

■ INGREDIENTS

- 2 lb (1 kg) lamb shoulder, with some loin attached
- ⅓ cup (3½ fl oz/100 ml) extra-virgin olive oil
- 3 cloves garlic (2 whole, 1 finely chopped)
- 2 tablespoons rosemary and sage, finely chopped
- salt and freshly ground black pepper
- ¾ cup (7 fl oz/200 ml) dry white wine
- 4 anchovy fillets, crumbled
- ½ cup (4 fl oz/125 ml) white vinegar

Wine: a dry red (Merlot di Aprilia)

Right: Abbacchio alla romana

Agnello con i piselli
Lamb stew with fresh rosemary, garlic, and peas

Serves: 6; Preparation: 10 minutes; Cooking: 1½ hours; Level of difficulty: Medium

Sauté the garlic, rosemary, and pancetta in a large sauté pan in the oil over medium heat for 4–5 minutes. § Add the lamb and season with salt and pepper. § Pour in the wine and cook until it has evaporated. § Stir in the tomatoes, lower heat, and partially cover the pan. Cook for about 50 minutes, stirring from time to time. § Remove the lamb from the pan, and set aside in a warm oven. Add the peas to the pan and sauté briefly in the sauce. § Add the lamb again and cook for 30 minutes more. § Serve hot with boiled rice and a mixed salad.

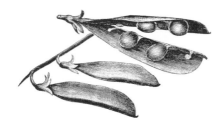

Cosciotto d'agnello alle erbe aromatiche
Roast leg of lamb with aromatic herbs

Serves: 4; Preparation: 10 minutes; Cooking: 1¾ hours; Level of difficulty: Simple

Cut the crusts off the bread and chop in a food processor with the garlic and aromatic herbs (leaves only). Season with salt and a generous grinding of pepper. § Put the butter in a roasting pan and place in a preheated oven at 375°F/190°C/gas 5 for a few minutes, until the butter melts. § Place the lamb in the roasting pan, drizzle with the oil, and scatter with the chopped herbs and bread. § Return to the oven and cook for 1½ hours, basting from time to time with the wine. § Transfer to a heated serving dish and serve hot. Carve the meat at the table. § Serve with roast, baked, or boiled potatoes and a mixed salad.

VARIATION
— Use the same ingredients and method to prepare a roast leg of turkey. Turkey has a less distinctive aroma than lamb which the herbs will enhance (whereas they tend to mellow and blend with the stronger taste of the lamb).

■ INGREDIENTS

- 2 cloves garlic, finely chopped
- 1 tablespoon rosemary, finely chopped
- ½ cup (2 oz/60 g) diced pancetta
- ⅓ cup (3½ fl oz/100 ml) extra-virgin olive oil
- 2½ lb (1.2 kg) lamb shoulder, cut into pieces, with bone
- salt and freshly ground black pepper
- ½ cup (4 fl oz/125 ml) dry white wine
- 3 tomatoes, peeled and chopped
- 3½ cups (1 lb/500 g) fresh or frozen shelled peas

Wine: a dry red (Barolo)

■ INGREDIENTS

- 3 slices sandwich bread
- 2 cloves garlic
- mixture of aromatic herbs: 4 leaves sage, 1 twig rosemary, 1 twig thyme, 1 twig marjoram, 1 large bunch parsley
- salt and freshly ground black pepper
- 2 tablespoons butter
- 2 lb (1 kg) leg of lamb
- 4 tablespoons extra-virgin olive oil
- ⅔ cup (5 fl oz/150 ml) dry white wine

Wine: a dry red (Rosso di Franciacorta)

Right: *Cosciotto d'agnello alle erbe aromatiche*

Agnello al latte
Lamb stewed in butter, brandy, rosemary, and milk

Serves: 6; Preparation: 15 minutes; Cooking: 1¼ hours; Level of difficulty: Medium

Dredge the lamb in the flour and then shake off any excess. § Melt the butter in a large, heavy-bottomed pan and sauté the pancetta for 2–3 minutes over medium heat. § Add the lamb, rosemary, salt, and pepper. § Sauté for 4–5 minutes, then pour in the brandy. Stir continuously until the brandy has evaporated. § Add the milk, partially cover the pan, and cook over medium-low heat, stirring often, for about 1 hour, or until the milk has reduced to a dense sauce. § Serve hot with a side dish of lightly boiled peas sautéed briefly in garlic, parsley, and oil.

■ INGREDIENTS

- 2½ lb (1.2 kg) lamb shoulder and leg, cut in pieces
- 1 cup (4 oz/125 g) all-purpose (plain) flour
- 2½ tablespoons butter
- 1 cup (4 oz/125 g) diced pancetta
- 1 tablespoon fresh rosemary, finely chopped
- salt and freshly ground black pepper
- ½ cup (4 fl oz/125 ml) brandy
- 2 cups (16 fl oz/500 ml) milk

Wine: a dry red (Bardolino Rosso)

Agnello al pomodoro
Hot and spicy tomato and lamb stew

Serves: 4-6; Preparation: 15 minutes; Cooking: 1¼ hours; Level of difficulty: Simple

Sauté the onion, carrot, celery, garlic, parsley, chillies, and pancetta over medium-high heat with the oil in a large, heavy-bottomed pan, preferably earthenware. § When the pancetta and onion are golden brown, add the lamb and cook with the vegetable mixture, stirring continuously, for 7–8 minutes more. § Season with salt and pepper and pour in the wine. Cook until the wine has evaporated. § Add the tomatoes, lower the heat to medium and partially cover. Cook for about 1 hour, adding a little hot water if the sauce reduces too much. § Serve hot with boiled rice, or boiled or baked potatoes, and a fresh green salad.

■ INGREDIENTS

- 1 onion, 1 carrot, 1 stalk celery, 2 cloves garlic, all finely chopped
- 2 tablespoons parsley, finely chopped
- 1 teaspoon chillies, crushed
- ½ cup (2 oz/60 g) diced pancetta
- 4 tablespoons extra-virgin olive oil
- 2¼ lb (1.2 kg) lamb, shoulder or leg, cut in pieces
- salt and freshly ground black pepper
- ⅔ cup (5 fl oz/150 ml) dry white wine
- 1 lb (500 g) peeled and chopped ripe tomatoes

Wine: a dry rosé (Cirò)

Right: *Costolette d'agnello fritte*

COSTOLETTE D'AGNELLO FRITTE
Breaded and fried lamb chops

■ INGREDIENTS

• 8 lamb chops

• salt

• ½ cup (2 oz/60 g) all-
  purpose (plain) flour

• 1 egg

• 1 cup (4 oz/125 g) bread
  crumbs

• ¾ cup (7 fl oz/200 ml)
  oil for frying

*Wine: a dry red
(Carmignano)*

Serves: 4; Preparation: 10 minutes; Cooking: 5-10 minutes; Level of difficulty: Simple

Pound the chops lightly to spread the meat as much as possible. § Sprinkle with salt, roll in the flour, and shake to remove excess. § Dip in the egg and coat well with the bread crumbs. § Heat the oil in a heavy-bottomed pan and fry the chops, turning them so that they are golden brown on both sides. § Drain on paper towels and serve very hot with a mixed platter of fried zucchini (courgettes), artichokes, and potatoes and a green salad.

SPEZZATINO D'AGNELLO E CARCIOFI IN FRICASSEA
Lamb and artichoke fricassee

■ INGREDIENTS

- 1¼ lb (600 g) lamb (boneless leg and shoulder), cut in pieces
- salt and freshly ground black pepper
- ½ cup (4 fl oz/125 ml) extra-virgin olive oil
- juice of 1½ lemons
- 3 globe artichokes
- 1½ cloves garlic, finely chopped
- ¾ cup (7 fl oz/200 ml) dry white wine
- ¾ cup (7 fl oz/200 ml) *Beef stock* (see recipe p. 22)
- 1 egg
- 1 tablespoon parsley, finely chopped

Wine: a dry white (Malvasia Secca del Carso)

Serves: 4; Preparation: 25 minutes + 2 hours to marinate the lamb; Cooking: 1¼ hours; Level of difficulty: Simple

Place the lamb in a bowl with salt, pepper, 4 tablespoons of oil, and the juice of half a lemon. Marinate for 2 hours. § Remove the tough outer leaves from the artichokes and trim the stalks and tops. Slice the tender inner hearts into segments. Wash in cold water and the juice of a lemon. § Heat 2 tablespoons of oil in a sauté pan over medium heat. Add the garlic and artichokes, sauté for 5–6 minutes, then set aside. § Drain the lamb thoroughly, and sauté in a separate heavy-bottomed pan with the remaining oil. § When the lamb is well browned, pour in the wine and cook until it evaporates. § Transfer the lamb to the sauté pan with the artichokes and season with salt to taste. § Partially cover the pan and cook over a medium heat for 1 hour, adding stock from time to time as the sauce reduces, and stirring frequently. § When the lamb is cooked, beat the egg with a little salt and the juice of half a lemon. Pour the egg mixture over the stew and turn off the heat. Toss carefully so that the egg cooks and sets. § Sprinkle with the parsley and serve hot.

AGNELLO ALL'AGRO
Lamb stewed in butter, oil, and white wine

■ INGREDIENTS

- 2½ lb (1.2 kg) lamb, leg or shoulder, cut in pieces
- 2 tablespoons butter
- 2 tablespoons extra-virgin olive oil
- salt and freshly ground black pepper
- ½ cup (4 fl oz/125 ml) dry white wine
- juice of 2 lemons

Wine: a robust, dry white (Donnafugata)

Serves: 6; Preparation: 10 minutes; Cooking: 1¾ hours; Level of difficulty: Simple

Sauté the lamb in the butter and oil over high heat in a large, heavy-bottomed pan. § Season with salt and pepper, mix well, and pour in half the wine and lemon juice. § Reduce heat to medium-low, partially cover the pan, and cook for about 1½ hours. Gradually stir in the remaining wine and lemon juice as the sauce reduces. § Serve hot with a side dish of lightly boiled Swiss chard sautéed briefly in extra-virgin olive oil with garlic, salt, pepper, and a little lemon juice.

Left: *Spezzatino d'agnello e carciofi in fricassea*

GAME

Many regional dishes are based on more unusual meats, such as rabbit, hare, wild boar, goat, and venison. The recipes in this chapter are a selection of the most popular ones.

Coniglio in fricassea
Rabbit fricassee

Serves: 4; Preparation: 15 minutes; Cooking: 1 hour; Level of difficulty: Simple

Rinse the rabbit under cold running water and pat dry with paper towels. § Cut into small pieces, roll in the flour and shake off any excess. § Sauté the onion in the butter and oil over medium-high heat in a large, heavy-bottomed pan until soft. § Add the rabbit and cook until the meat is white (not brown). § Pour in the wine and cook until it evaporates. Season with salt and pepper. § Reduce the heat, partially cover and cook for about 40 minutes, adding the stock gradually as the sauce reduces. § When the rabbit is cooked, beat the egg yolks in a bowl with the lemon juice and parsley. Pour the mixture over the rabbit and turn off the heat. Toss carefully so that the egg cooks and sets. § Serve hot with lightly boiled globe artichokes briefly sautéed in garlic, olive oil, and parsley.

> VARIATIONS
> – For a tastier dish, replace the butter with the same quantity of lard.
> – For a different but equally delicious dish, replace the rabbit with the same quantity of chicken.

INGREDIENTS

- 1 rabbit, about 2½ lb (1.2 kg)
- 2 tablespoons all-purpose (plain) flour
- 1 onion, thinly sliced
- 2 tablespoons butter
- 4 tablespoons extra-virgin olive oil
- ½ cup (4 fl oz/125 ml) dry white wine
- salt and freshly ground black pepper
- 1 cup (8 fl oz/250 ml) *Beef stock* (see recipe p. 22)
- 1 tablespoon parsley, finely chopped
- 2 egg yolks, very fresh
- juice of 1 lemon

Wine: a dry white (Galestro)

Rotolo di coniglio in porchetta
Crispy, rolled roast rabbit

Serves: 6; Preparation: 15 minutes; Cooking: 1 hour; Level of difficulty: Simple

Open the rabbit out into a single flat slice and lightly beat with a meat pounder. § Season with salt and pepper and sprinkle with the herbs, garlic, and fennel seeds. § Roll the rabbit up and tie with kitchen string. § Place in an ovenproof dish with the oil and bake in a preheated oven at 400°F/200°C/gas 6 for 1 hour. Turn the rabbit from time to time during cooking and baste with the wine so that the meat does not become too dry. If the wine is insufficient, add a little more (or, alternatively, add a little beef stock). § Slice the roast rabbit and serve hot with a green salad. Serve the cooking juices separately.

INGREDIENTS

- 2½ lb (1.2 kg) boneless rabbit
- salt and freshly ground black pepper
- 2 tablespoons aromatic herbs (thyme, sage, rosemary), finely chopped
- 2 cloves garlic, finely chopped
- 1 teaspoon fennel seeds
- 4 tablespoons extra-virgin olive oil
- ½ cup (4 fl oz/125 ml) dry white wine

Wine: a dry white (Rosso di Gallura)

Right: Rotolo di coniglio in porchetta

■ INGREDIENTS

- 1 rabbit, about 2½ lb (1.2 kg), cut in pieces
- 4 tablespoons extra-virgin olive oil
- 1 clove garlic, finely chopped
- salt and freshly ground black pepper
- ½ cup (4 fl oz/125 ml) dry white wine
- ¾ cup (7 fl oz/200 ml) Beef stock (see recipe p. 22)
- 1 cup (3½ oz/100 g) green olives
- ⅓ cup (2 oz/60 g) pine nuts

Wine: a dry white
(Trebbiano d'Abruzzo)

Spezzatino di coniglio ai pinoli e olive verdi
Rabbit stew with pine nuts and green olives

Serves: 6; Preparation: 10 minutes; Cooking: 1 hour; Level of difficulty: Simple

Rinse the rabbit under cold running water and pat dry with paper towels. § Heat the oil in a large, heavy-bottomed pan over medium heat and sauté the garlic for 1–2 minutes. § Add the rabbit, sprinkle with salt and pepper, and brown all over. § Pour in the wine and cook until it has evaporated. § Reduce the heat to medium-low, partially cover and cook for 40 minutes, adding the stock gradually as the meat dries out. You may not need to add it all. § Add the olives and pine nuts and cook for 15 minutes more. The rabbit should be very tender. § Serve hot with boiled potatoes or rice.

■ INGREDIENTS

- 1 boned rabbit, about 2 lb (1 kg)
- 1 tablespoon sage and rosemary, finely chopped
- 1 clove garlic, finely chopped
- salt and freshly ground black pepper
- 4 tablespoons extra-virgin olive oil
- 2 eggs
- 1 rabbit liver, coarsely chopped
- 1 chicken liver, coarsely chopped
- ½ cup (4 fl oz/125 ml) dry white wine

Wine: a dry red
(San Severo Rosso)

Coniglio dissosato all'antica
Old-fashioned boned rabbit

Serves: 4-6; Preparation: 25 minutes; Cooking: 1 hour; Level of difficulty: Medium

Open the rabbit out into a single flat slice and lightly beat with a meat pounder. § Sprinkle with the sage, rosemary, garlic, salt, and pepper. § Beat the eggs in a bowl with a little salt. § Heat 1 tablespoon of oil in a sauté pan and cook the eggs until firm. § Place the cooked eggs over the rabbit. Sprinkle with the livers and salt to taste. § Roll the rabbit up and tie with kitchen string. Place in a roasting pan with the remaining oil and bake in a preheated oven at 400°F/200°C/gas 6 for 1 hour. Turn from time to time, basting with the wine so that the meat does not dry out. If the wine is insufficient, add a little more (or, alternatively, use a little beef stock). § Cut the rabbit into thick slices and transfer to a heated serving dish. Serve hot, with the cooking juices served separately. Serve with lightly boiled broccoli or chopped cabbage, sautéed briefly in extra-virgin olive oil with garlic and crushed chillies.

Left: *Spezzatino di coniglio ai pinoli e olive verdi*

LEPRE BRASATA AL VINO ROSSO
Braised hare in red wine sauce

Serves: 8; Preparation: 40 minutes + 8 hours marinating; Cooking: 2 hours; Level of difficulty: Medium

Place the hare in a large bowl with the red wine, celery, carrot, onion, rosemary, sage, bay leaves, garlic, and juniper berries. Set aside to marinate for at least 8 hours. § Drain the marinade from the hare. Set the liquid aside for cooking and finely chop the celery, carrot, onion, and garlic. Set the bunch of herbs aside. § Heat the oil and butter over medium heat in a heavy-bottomed pan, add the vegetables, and sauté for 5–7 minutes. § Lightly flour the pieces of hare and add them to the vegetables. Add the bunch of herbs and sauté for 5–10 minutes. § Pour in the wine and cook until it has evaporated. Season with salt and pepper to taste. § Add the tomato paste, tomatoes, and hot water. Partially cover and cook for 1¾ hours, or until the hare is very tender. Stir from time to time. § Discard the bunch of herbs. § Serve on a bed of potato purée.

■ INGREDIENTS
- 1 hare, about 4 lb (2 kg), cut in pieces
- 2 cups (16 fl oz/500 ml) red wine
- 1 stalk celery, 1 carrot, 1 onion, all coarsely chopped
- 1 twig rosemary, 1 twig sage, 3 bay leaves, all tied together in a bunch
- 2 cloves garlic, whole
- 1 teaspoon juniper berries
- ⅓ cup (3½ fl oz/100 ml) extra-virgin olive oil
- 2 tablespoons butter
- 2 tablespoons all-purpose (plain) flour
- salt and freshly ground black pepper
- 3 tablespoons tomato paste
- 12 oz (350 g) tomatoes, peeled and chopped
- ½ cup (4 fl oz/125 ml) hot water

Wine: a dry red (Aglianico di Vulcano)

PICCIONE RIPIENO AI FEGATINI
Roast pigeon stuffed with sausage and liver

Serves: 4; Preparation: 25 minutes; Cooking: 45 minutes; Level of difficulty: Simple

Clean the pigeons, discarding all internal organs except the livers. Wash the pigeons under cold running water and pat dry with paper towels. § Chop the pigeon livers with the chicken livers and sausages on a cutting board using a heavy, well-sharpened knife. § Transfer the sausage and liver mixture to a bowl. Season with salt and pepper and mix well. § Fill each pigeon with the stuffing and close them up with toothpicks, or by sewing with a needle and kitchen thread. § Fix 2 leaves of sage to each pigeon with a toothpick. § Sprinkle the birds with salt and pepper and place in a roasting pan. Drizzle with the oil and roast in a preheated oven at 375°F/190°C/gas 5 for 45 minutes. § Serve hot with a side dish of lightly boiled zucchini (courgettes) or Brussels sprouts briefly sautéed in garlic, parsley, and olive oil.

■ INGREDIENTS
- 4 squab pigeons, with their livers
- 2 chicken livers
- 2 Italian pork sausages
- salt and freshly ground black pepper
- 8 leaves sage
- ⅓ cup (3½ fl oz/100 ml) extra-virgin olive oil

Wine: a dry red (Colli Piacentini Bonarda)

Right: *Lepre brasata al vino rosso*

Cinghiale in bianco ai porri
Wild boar and leek stew

Serves: 6; Preparation: 15 minutes + 24 hours marinating; Cooking: 2¾ hours; Level of difficulty: Medium

Place the wild boar in a large bowl with the wine, cloves, and bay leaves. Sprinkle with salt and pepper and set aside to marinate for at least 24 hours. § Drain the marinade from the wild boar. Set the liquid aside for cooking and discard the cloves and bay leaves. § Heat the oil in a large, heavy-bottomed pan over medium heat and sauté the prosciutto for 1–2 minutes. § Add the leeks and a ladleful of stock and cook until the leeks begin to soften. § Add the meat and gently brown all over. § Pour in the liquid from the marinade, partially cover the pan, and cook for about 2½ hours, adding stock so that the meat doesn't dry out. § When the meat is tender, add the vinegar and pine nuts and stir well. Dissolve the flour in 2 tablespoons of cold water and stir into the sauce until it thickens. § Serve the stew hot on polenta or with baked or boiled potatoes.

■ INGREDIENTS

• 2 lb (1 kg) wild boar, in pieces
• 4 cups (2 pints/1 liter) dry white wine
• 3 cloves
• 2 bay leaves
• salt and freshly ground black pepper
• ⅓ cup (3½ fl oz/100 ml) extra-virgin olive oil
• 1 cup (4 oz/125 g) chopped prosciutto
• 3 leeks, in thin slices
• 2 cups (16 fl oz/500 ml) *Beef stock* (see recipe p. 22)
• 4 tablespoons white vinegar
• 1 teaspoon pine nuts
• 1 tablespoon all-purpose (plain) flour

Wine: a dry red (Morellino di Scansano)

Cinghiale stufato
Wild boar in red wine and tomato sauce

Wild boar has a very strong and distinctive taste. To enjoy it at its best, it should be marinated for at least 12 hours before cooking. I prefer to leave it for a full day before use. This delicious stew is traditionally served with hot polenta.

Serves: 6; Preparation: 30 minutes; Cooking: 2¼ hours + 24 hours marinating; Level of difficulty: Medium

Place the wild boar in a large bowl with the onion, carrot, celery, garlic, cloves, bay leaves, salt, and pepper. Cover with the wine and set aside to marinate for 12–24 hours. § Drain the marinade from the wild boar. Set the liquid aside for cooking, discard the cloves and bay leaves, and coarsely chop the vegetables. § Heat the oil in a large, heavy-bottomed pan over medium heat and sauté the vegetables for 5–7 minutes. § Add the meat and sauté until brown all over. § Add the tomato sauce, stir well and pour in the liquid from the marinade. Partially cover the pan and cook over medium-low heat for 2 hours, stirring from time to time. When cooked, the wild boar should be tender and the sauce quite thick. § Serve hot on freshly-made polenta.

VARIATION
– For a milder stew, do not reuse the vegetables from the marinade; replace with equal quantities of fresh chopped vegetables.

■ INGREDIENTS

• 2¾ lb (1.3 kg) wild boar, cut in pieces
• 1 onion, sliced
• 1 carrot, thickly sliced
• 1 stalk celery, thickly sliced
• 1 clove garlic, cut in half
• 2 cloves
• 2 bay leaves
• 1 cup (8 fl oz/250 ml) robust red wine
• ⅓ cup (3½ fl oz/100 ml) extra virgin olive oil
• ½ quantity *Simple tomato sauce* (see recipe p. 16)
• salt and freshly ground black pepper

Wine: a dry red (Barbaresco)

Right: *Cinghiale in bianco ai porri*

Nana con polpettine di sedano alla figlinese
Duck with celery balls

Serves: 4; Preparation: 40 minutes; Cooking: 1½ hours; Level of difficulty: Medium

Sear the duck and cut into pieces. § Sauté the chopped vegetables with the oil in a heavy-bottomed pan over medium heat. § After about 5 minutes, add the duck. Season with salt and pepper and continue cooking until the duck is brown. § Pour in the wine and cook until it evaporates. § Stir in the tomatoes, partially cover the pan, and simmer for about 1½ hours. Stir frequently, gradually adding the stock as the sauce reduces. § In the meantime, wash the celery stalks and cut into large pieces. Boil in a little salted water for 25–30 minutes. Drain well, squeeze out excess moisture and chop (not too finely). § Shape the celery into small balls, dip in the flour, then the egg. § Fry the celery balls in the oil in a heavy-bottomed pan over medium heat. Drain and set aside on paper towels. § Add the celery balls to the duck during the last 15 minutes of cooking. Take care when stirring or the balls may come apart. § Serve hot.

■ INGREDIENTS

- 1 duck, cleaned, about 2 lb (1 kg)
- 1 clove garlic, 1 onion, 1 stalk celery, 1 carrot, all finely chopped
- 1 lb (500 g) tomatoes, peeled and chopped
- ½ cup (4 fl oz/125 ml) robust dry red wine
- 2 cups (16 fl oz/500 ml) *Beef stock* (see recipe p. 22)
- ⅓ cup (3½ fl oz/100 ml) extra-virgin olive oil
- salt and freshly ground black pepper
- 2 large stalks celery
- ¾ cup (3 oz/90 g) all-purpose (plain) flour
- 1 egg, beaten
- ¾ cup (7 fl oz/200 ml) olive oil for frying

*Wine: a dry red
(Chianti Classico Santa Cristina)*

Petto d'anatra all'arancia
Duck breast with orange sauce

Serves: 4; Preparation: 20 minutes; Cooking: 25 minutes; Level of difficulty: Simple

Wash the duck under cold running water and pat dry with paper towels. § Place in a roasting dish with the oil. Sprinkle with salt and pepper and bake in a preheated oven at 400°F/200°C/gas 6 for 20–30 minutes. § When cooked, set the duck aside in a warm oven. § Peel the orange and cut the peel in thin strips. § Put the peel in a pot of boiling water for 1 minute then drain. Remove the peel with a slotted spoon, wait for the water to boil again, and repeat the process. This will take the bitter taste out of the peel. § Squeeze the orange and strain the juice. § Skim the fat from the juices in the roasting pan. Place the pan over medium heat and add the cognac and orange juice. After a few minutes add the sugar and salt to taste. Boil for 3–4 minutes then add the orange peel. § Slice the duck thinly and arrange on a heated serving dish. Spoon the sauce over the top. § Serve hot with potato purée.

■ INGREDIENTS

- 1¼ lb (600 g) duck breast
- 4 tablespoons extra-virgin olive oil
- salt and freshly ground black pepper
- 1 orange
- ½ cup (4 fl oz/125 ml) dry red wine
- 2 teaspoons castor sugar

*Wine: a dry white
(Bianco di Custoza)*

Right:
Petto d'anatra all'arancia

Quagliette bardate alla pancetta
Quails wrapped with pancetta

■ INGREDIENTS

• 6 quails
• salt and freshly ground black pepper
• 12 slices pancetta
• 1 carrot, 1 stalk celery, finely chopped
• 2 oz (60 g) prosciutto, finely chopped
• 1 scallion (shallot), coarsely chopped
• 1 bay leaf
• 2 juniper berries
• ½ cup (4 fl oz/125 ml) dry white wine
• 1 cup (8 fl oz/250 ml) *Beef stock* (see recipe p. 22)
• salt and freshly ground black pepper
• 4 tablespoons extra-virgin olive oil

Wine: a dry red
(Brunello di Montalcino)

Serves: 6; Preparation: 30 minutes; Cooking: 45 minutes; Level of difficulty: Simple

Remove the heads from the quails, and sear to eliminate any remaining plumage. § Sprinkle the quail with salt and pepper. Wrap each bird with 2 slices of pancetta and tie with kitchen string. § Place in a baking dish with the oil, carrot, celery, and prosciutto. Add the bay leaf and juniper berries and scatter the scallion over the top. § Bake in a preheated oven at 400°F/200°C/gas 6 for about 45 minutes. § Pour the wine over the quails during cooking. When the wine is finished, continue with the stock. § Serve the quails hot with their sauce spooned over the top. § Serve with zucchini (courgettes), cut thinly lengthways, and sautéed for a few minutes in olive oil, finely chopped garlic, and parsley.

Anatra agli aromi
Roast duck with herbs

■ INGREDIENTS

• 1 large onion
• 1 duck, about 2 lb (1 kg)
• 1 bay leaf
• mixed sprigs fresh herbs: sage, rosemary, thyme, marjoram
• salt
• 4 tablespoons extra-virgin olive oil
• 1 tablespoon pink pepper
• ½ cup (4 fl oz/125 ml) dry white wine
• ½ cup (4 fl oz/125 ml) white vinegar
• 1 chicken stock cube

Wine: a dry white
(Sauvignon di Parma)

Serves: 4; Preparation: 10 minutes; Cooking: about 1 hour; Level of difficulty: Simple

Peel and wash the onion, leaving it whole. Stick with the bay leaf and the other sprigs of herbs so that they will not come out during cooking. § Clean and sear the duck to eliminate any remaining plumage. § Place in a roasting pan and sprinkle with the salt and oil. § Add the onion, crumbled stock cube, and pink pepper. § Bake in a preheated oven at 400°F/200°C/gas 6. § After about 10 minutes, pour the wine and vinegar over the top. Cook for about 50 minutes more, basting from time to time. § Cut the duck into small pieces and arrange them on a heated serving dish with the chopped onion and herbs. § Serve hot with Swiss chard (silver beet) lightly boiled in salted water and briefly sautéed in olive oil and finely chopped garlic.

Left: *Quagliette bardate alla pancetta*

Capriolo marinato all'aceto
Venison marinated with vinegar

Serves: 6; Preparation: 30 minutes + 24 hours marinating; Cooking: 2½ hours; Level of difficulty: Medium

Sauté the garlic, onion, carrot, celery, parsley, thyme, and peppercorns in the oil over medium-high heat. § Sprinkle with salt and pour in the wine and vinegar. Cook for 20 minutes. § Chop the sautéed mixture in a food processor. § Combine the puréed mixture in a bowl with the venison. If the mixture is too thick, add a little more white wine and 1 tablespoon of extra-virgin olive oil. § Stir well and set aside to marinate for 24 hours. § Drain the venison from the marinade. Set the marinade aside in a bowl. § Sauté the pancetta in the lard (or butter) in a large, heavy-bottomed pan for a few minutes. § Add the venison, season with salt and pepper, partially cover, and cook over low heat for about 2½ hours. Stir frequently, gradually adding the marinade and the the stock. § Serve hot with freshly-made polenta.

Fagiano alle olive nere
Pheasant with black olives

Serves: 4; Preparation: 15 minutes; Cooking: 1¼ hours; Level of difficulty: Simple

Clean and sear the pheasant to eliminate any remaining plumage. § Season with salt and pepper inside and out. Sprinkle with flour and shake to remove any excess. § Sauté the onion in the oil in a large, heavy-bottomed pan. § Add the pheasant and sauté for a few minutes. § Pour in the wine and cook until it evaporates. § Stir in the tomatoes and season with salt. Partially cover and cook over medium heat for about 45 minutes. Gradually add the stock as the sauce reduces. § Add the olives, stir well and cook for 15 minutes more. § Remove the pheasant from the pan and cut into pieces. Return to the sauce to reheat over medium heat. § Arrange on a heated serving dish. Serve hot with lightly boiled spinach briefly sautéed in olive oil and finely chopped garlic.

■ INGREDIENTS

- 1 clove garlic, 1 onion, finely chopped
- 1 carrot, cut in wheels
- 1 stalk celery, sliced
- 1 tablespoon parsley, finely chopped
- 1 tablespoon thyme, finely chopped
- 6–8 peppercorns
- ⅓ cup (3½ fl oz/100 ml) extra-virgin olive oil
- salt and freshly ground black pepper
- ¾ cup (7 fl oz/200 ml) dry white wine
- ½ cup (4 fl oz/125 ml) white vinegar
- 2 lb (1 kg) venison
- ½ cup (5 oz/150 g) diced pancetta
- 4 tablespoons lard or butter
- 2 cups (16 fl oz/500 ml) *Beef stock (see recipe p. 22)*

Wine: a dry red (Chianti Classico)

■ INGREDIENTS

- 1 pheasant, about 2 lb (1 kg)
- 1 large white onion, sliced
- 1 cup (3½ oz/100 g) black olives
- 4 tablespoons all-purpose (plain) flour
- 14 oz (450 g) tomatoes, peeled and chopped
- ⅓ cup (3½ fl oz/100 ml) extra-virgin olive oil
- ¾ cup (7 fl oz/200 ml) dry white wine
- ¾ cup (7 fl oz/200 ml) *Beef stock (see recipe p. 22)*
- salt and freshly ground black pepper

Wine: a dry red (Barolo)

Right: *Fagiano alle olive nere*

Index